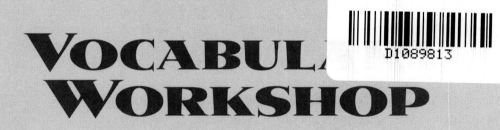

VOCABULARY WORKSHOP

LEVEL BLUE

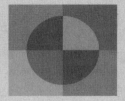

Teacher's Annotated Edition

With Answers to Tests (Cycles One and Two)

SADLIER-OXFORD

A Division of William H. Sadlier, Inc.

New York, NY 10005-1002

VOCABULARY WORKSHOP

THE CLASSIC PROGRAM FOR:

- developing and enriching vocabulary resources
- promoting more effective communication in today's world
- improving vocabulary skills assessed
  on standardized tests

Printed in the United States of America
ISBN: 0-8215-0415-0
3456789/01 00 99

CONTENTS

INTRODUCTION

Over the last five decades VOCABULARY WORKSHOP has become the "classic" program for

- guiding and stimulating vocabulary growth in Grades 6–12;
- preparing students in those grades for vocabulary-related exercises found in tests.

Level Blue, one of two new additions to the VOCABULARY WORKSHOP series

- extends the program to students in the upper elementary grades, and increases the range of levels suitable for use by middle school students;
- faithfully maintains the approach that has made VOCABULARY WORKSHOP so beneficial;
- introduces new features to keep abreast of changing times and changing testing procedures, particularly in regard to standardized tests.

This Teacher's Edition for Level Blue of VOCABULARY WORKSHOP is designed to help teachers make effective use of the program in the classroom.

- Part I furnishes teachers with an overview of the goals, grade placements, and pedagogical approach of the VOCABULARY WORKSHOP program.
- Part II familiarizes teachers with the Student Text and Supplementary Testing Program for this level and outlines a plan for the integrated use of these items during the school year.
- Part III provides practical suggestions for effectively implementing the program in the classroom.

OVERVIEW

Goals

The goals of the VOCABULARY WORKSHOP program are threefold:

- developing and enhancing student vocabulary resources;

- promoting more effective communication, both oral and written, in today's world;

- improving vocabulary-related skills assessed on standardized tests.

Grade-Level Placement

Level Blue has been conceived with the fifth grader in mind, Level Orange with the fourth grader.

In determining "proper" placement of either level in a given situation, however, the following considerations should be taken into account:

- Grade levels indicated should not be taken in too literal or rigorous a sense. A certain amount of experimentation, as well as the use of the Diagnostic Test, are needed to establish the "correct" placement of a particular level in a given situation.

- Both Levels Blue and Orange have been prepared in such a way as to offer *some* students in grades 6 and 7 with material as challenging, though different in format, as the first two levels of the VOCABULARY WORKSHOP Levels A–H.

- Differences in grade are reflected not only in the "difficulty" of the words presented but also in the "maturity" of the sentences and other contexts in which those words are used.

Pedagogical Approach

VOCABULARY WORKSHOP features a *balanced approach* to word acquisition.

- This approach focuses primarily on the words themselves, their meanings, their ranges of application (applicability), and their relationships to other words.

- At the same time, the approach recognizes the importance of textual *context* in the acquisition of vocabulary and in its proper usage.

One of the cornerstones of the pedagogical approach taken in VOCABULARY WORKSHOP is intensive reinforcement through varied and abundant "hands-on" exercises. This method of teaching vocabulary is emphasized to provide students with

- maximum exposure to different meanings of the key words studied;

- maximum coverage of the range of applicability of each key word through its application in the greatest possible number of different contexts;

- fullest understanding of a key word's relationships to other words.

Although it is customary to say that a student does or does not "know" a particular word, it should be recognized that there are actually many levels of word recognition and control.

These levels range from complete nonrecognition to partial or complete recognition *in context only* to the full incorporation of a word in a student's active vocabulary.

The aim of the instructional material and exercises presented in VOCABULARY WORKSHOP is to move the word into the students' active daily-use vocabulary.

A Consumable Program

A major feature of this program is that the students are directed to write answers directly in the book. This technique was designed to

- help students learn to spell the key words properly;

- ensure active student participation in the program;

- build a permanent record of student work.

Word Lists

The Student Texts for Levels Blue and Orange each contain 192 key words, divided over 16 Units.

Criteria for Selection

The selection of words was based on four major criteria:

- currency in and usefulness for present-day American oral and written communication;

- frequency on recognized vocabulary and spelling lists;

- applicability to standardized tests;

- current grade-placement research.

General Sources

The lists of key words were developed from many sources:

- traditional, classic, and contemporary fiction and nonfiction, including novels, short stories, biographies, essays, newspaper and magazine articles, plays, films, videos, TV programs;

- spelling and vocabulary lists recognized as valid bases for teaching language skills;

- current subject-area textbooks, glossaries, and ancillary materials (especially for general, nontechnical terms).

Dictionary and Reference Sources

The following were the primary dictionary resources used for word (and definition) selection:

- *Webster's Third International Dictionary of the English Language* (unabridged);

- *Merriam-Webster's Collegiate Dictionary* (tenth edition).

Other dictionary reference works consulted include:

- *The American Heritage Dictionary of the English Language* (all three editions);
- *The Random House Dictionary of the English Language* (unabridged; both editions);
- *The Compact Edition of the Oxford English Dictionary.*

In addition, a number of other word finders or reference works were utilized in preparing the drill, testing, reinforcement, or enhancement materials.

Standard Word-Frequency Sources

Standard word-frequency studies were employed to evaluate and revise the words on the tentative lists. These include:

Dale-O'Rourke: *The Living Word Vocabulary*

Carroll-Davies-Richman: *Word Frequency Book*

Zeno-Ivens-Millard-Duvvuri: *The Educator's Word Frequency Guide*

Harris-Jacobsen: *Basic Reading Vocabularies*

In compiling word lists, every effort has been made to include only such words as, according to authorities consulted, are not yet generally known at the grade for which the level has been prepared. The word list for Level Blue, for example, is comprised largely of words not known (again, according to the sources consulted) until at least sixth, seventh, or even eighth grade. From time to time, an exception has been made for a word on the basis of its appearance in standardized testing or in the curriculum at a specific grade.

The VOCABULARY WORKSHOP Program for Levels A–H

The Student Texts and Supplementary Testing Programs for Levels Blue and Orange are based on the same principles as, and are in many respects similar to, their counterparts at Levels A–H (grades 6–12+). There are some differences, however, in the number and types of components. Those for the program at Levels A–H are as follows:

- Student Texts, 8 Levels (A–H)
- Answer Keys, 8 Levels (A–H)
- Supplementary Testing Program
  - — Cycle One, 8 Levels (A–H)
  - — Cycle Two, 8 Levels (A–H)
  - — Combined Answer Keys, 8 Levels (A–H)
- SAT-Type TEST PREP Blackline Masters (answers included), 8 Levels (A–H)
- Interactive Audio Pronunciation Program, 6 Levels (A–F)
- Series Teacher's Guide, 1 volume

PROGRAM COMPONENTS FOR LEVEL BLUE

Level Blue of VOCABULARY WORKSHOP consists of the following components:

- Student Text
- Supplementary Testing Program (Cycles One and Two)
- Teacher's Annotated Edition

The Student Text may be used alone or in conjunction with the Supplementary Testing Program. A suggested schedule for the year (based on 25 weeks) on pages xiv–xv provides an outline of how the Student Text and Supplementary Testing Program might be integrated.

THE STUDENT TEXT

Introductory Materials

The Vocabulary of Vocabulary

At the beginning of each Student Text there is a special section called *The Vocabulary of Vocabulary*. It has been provided to give students some useful concepts and terminology that they will apply throughout the VOCABULARY WORKSHOP program.

Many students will already be familiar with parts of speech and with synonyms and antonyms. The simple exercises that follow these two sections (see student pages 5 and 6) should be sufficient to clarify and consolidate this material.

The sections on Context Clues and Analogies (student pages 7 and 8) may require more time and attention, depending on the student's familiarity with these concepts and comfort with these skills.

The Diagnostic Test

After completing work on *The Vocabulary of Vocabulary,* it is advisable that the teacher assess the students' overall vocabulary and test-taking skills. The *Diagnostic Test* on student pages 10–11 has been provided for this purpose.

The Diagnostic Test allows for flexible use.

- It can be applied to give an *initial assessment* of the challenge that lies ahead.
- It also serves to give a *before-and-after comparison* when combined with the Final Mastery Test.

Although the Diagnostic Test may be presented as a timed speed test, with the specific aim of determining how many items students can answer in 10 to 15 minutes, it is better used as an informal motivational device. Speed will come when interest and mastery have been developed.

The Units

Having completed the preliminaries indicated above and made some assessment of the task ahead, the teacher is ready to take on the main work of the year, the study of the 192 key words presented in the 16 Units of each Student Text.

Structure of the Unit

The work of each Unit is divided into a unique *5-part structure* designed to give maximum coverage to each of the key words within the space available.

Definitions and Related Matters

1. Definitions The *definitions* provided are *not of the dictionary* type. They are, for the most part, relatively brief and simple. The intent is to give students a reasonably good "core" idea of what each word means, without extensive detail or secondary connotations.

Generally, only a single meaning of maximum usefulness is given. However, several meanings may be indicated if they are distinct or if they appear to be more or less equally useful.

- The **part of speech** of each word is indicated at the beginning of the definition, using a simple set of abbreviations. When a word functions as several parts of speech, the appropriate abbreviation appears before the corresponding definition.

- With each word listing, the **pronunciation** is indicated by means of a simple set of diacritical marks presented at the beginning of every Student Text (see student page 9).

  The practice has been to indicate *only one pronunciation*, even where alternate pronunciations are sanctioned by the dictionary. There are only a few exceptions to this — mostly when a word changes its pronunciation in accordance with its use as different parts of speech.

- After each definition, the student is required to write the word in a blank space in an **illustrative sentence**. This offers no problem of selection, but it does focus attention on the illustrative sentence, and the act of writing is in itself a form of reinforcement. Also, writing out the word provides a good opportunity to focus attention on the spelling of the words.

  It should be noted that the illustrative sentences provide a *context* that clarifies the meaning of each word and points out its idiomatic usage. By writing the word in such contextual settings, students begin to see how it can be used effectively in their own communication. In most cases, nouns appear in the singular and verbs in the present tense.

- The illustrative sentence is followed by a list of **synonyms** and **antonyms** (for those words that have either or both). The lists are not meant to be exhaustive, and care has been taken not to include legitimate but obscure synonyms or antonyms. The point of these lists is to familiarize the students with thesaurus clusters of which the target words are part.

2. Match the Meaning Following the definitions is a set of exercises designed to reinforce the students' understanding and recall of the meanings. In *Match the Meaning* the students must choose from four taught words (all of the same part of speech) the word indicated by the clue, which is usually formulated as an abridged version or paraphrase of the definition.

3. Synonyms and Antonyms In the *Synonyms and Antonyms* exercises students must select the taught word that is synonym (or antonym) to a highlighted word in an illustrative phrase. If an antonym, the highlighted word is one listed as such in the *Definitions* section; if a synonym, the word is either part of the definition or listed as a synonym in the *Definitions* section. Each of the 12 unit words is used once in either the *Synonyms* or *Antonyms*.

4. Completing the Sentence The next section is a completion exercise in which students are asked to choose and write the word from the unit that logically and meaningfully fits into a blank in a given sentence. Each word in a unit is used once. Students should be alerted to the fact that nouns may be used either in singular or plural, and that verbs may be used in any tense or form (participial, for example), as required by the sentence.

The items in this exercise are organized in groups, or clusters, of no fewer than three and no more than six, and are related by theme or subject matter. Most of the items consist of a single sentence, but a few extend to two. The clusters cover topics in history, geography, civics, science, and the arts, as well as many others of interest or relevance to the students.

Students are expected to use context clues within sentences or groups of sentences to choose the correct word for each item. (For more on context clues, see *The Vocabulary of Vocabulary,* page 5.) This exercise is designed in such a way as to give students practice both in using context as a guide to correct usage and word selection, and in developing test-taking strategies such as "process of elimination."

5. Word Associations The last section is a set of exercises challenging the students to *apply* what they have learned of the words in a way that calls for a measure of perception and imagination. It is expected that by this point the students will have absorbed the meanings and become familiar with the usage of the words. In *Word Associations* the students are asked to go one step further and demonstrate their knowledge by choosing the answer that best completes a sentence or answers a question highlighting the taught word.

Follow-up and Enrichment Activities

Cursive Practice
Students who require practice in cursive might copy the unit words in cursive handwriting on a separate sheet of paper or in a vocabulary journal.

Sentence Framing
Students who find it difficult to use unit words correctly might be given practice, either in class or as homework, in writing sentences of their own devising. These can be checked and corrected by the teacher or, if it seems advisable, by a peer.

Creative Writing
Most students enjoy writing. Accordingly, at the conclusion of work on a unit, students might be invited to create their own original stories or essays using a given number of key words they have just studied.

Unit Tests (Optional Purchase)
Once the work of the Unit in the Student Text has been completed, the teacher may administer the corresponding Unit Test in the Supplementary Testing Program (see p. xiii below).

The Reviews and Cumulative Reviews

A Review appears after each sequence of four Units, and covers only the words taught in those four units.

All four Reviews follow the same organization and feature the same sets of exercises, excepting the last set in each. **Word Games**, which concludes each review, differs from one to the next.

The Reviews begin with **Selecting Word Meanings**, which has the students match a taught word with a synonym or synonymous phrase. Next is **Spelling**. In this exercise students must first decide if a letter is missing from a taught word and, if one is missing, to supply it. Note that in no case is a word presented as deliberately misspelled. **Antonyms** is fashioned as in the units, with this difference: that in the Reviews the taught unit word, rather than a taught antonym, is given in the introductory phrase.

The two sections that follow, **Vocabulary in Context** and **Analogies**, have been included to provide further review and to give students practice in skills commonly assessed in standardized tests.

Vocabulary in Context is a cloze exercise that has students supply missing words in a passage. Although it is similar in some respects to **Completing the Sentence** (see p. x above), it differs in important ways: the passage flows uninterrupted, as in many standardized tests; it relies more on general context rather than restatement and contrast clues to point the students to the correct answers; and in format it approximates that found in many standardized tests.

The questions that conclude the exercise act as "tests" with which students can check their choices, and provide opportunities for the students themselves to use the words in sentences of their own devising.

The **Analogies** are valuable not merely as a kind of mental gymnastics but also as a means of pinning down the exact meanings of words and of correcting misconceptions or uncertainties about how those words are used. Analogies also provide an excellent means for cultivating and refining critical-thinking skills.

It is impossible, of course, to catalog all the relationships that may be embodied in analogy questions. They are as open-ended as the mental capacity to manipulate ideas and terms. The types of analogies found in the Reviews, however, have been kept to a number and to a degree of difficulty thought to be manageable by students at grades 4-6. Most of the analogies are of a purely vocabulary-based nature; that is, the relationship between the key words is either that of synonyms or antonyms.

Each of the **Analogies** exercises concludes with a "Challenge" item asking students to write a comparison based on given words. All of the analogies that may be made from the words, as well as explanations of the relationships, can be found on p. xxiv of this Guide.

The **Word Families** section has been designed to help students expand and enrich their vocabularies by building upon the words presented in the units.

Word Games, which concludes the Review, presents a final reinforcement of usage and meaning in the form of a game or puzzle.

Cumulative Reviews

Two Cumulative Reviews have been provided in the Student Text, one following the Review for Units 5–8 and one following the Review for Units 13–16. Cumulative Review I covers the words presented in the first half of the book (Units 1–8), and Cumulative Review II covers the words presented in the second half (Units 9–16).

The sets of exercises included in the Cumulative Reviews are straightforward in nature, and in format have been designed in such a way as to maximize the number of words to be reviewed. In the **Definitions** and **Antonyms** sections students must match definitions and antonyms to taught words. **Completing the Sentence** is similar in purpose to the corresponding exercise in the Units, but in the Cumulative Reviews students are given a limited number of words from which to choose, and the sentences are not thematically related.

The **Classifying** exercise is unique to the Cumulative Reviews. This exercise challenges the students to look at the taught words from new and interesting perspectives, to recognize relationships between words, and to see as well that these words may be considered as members of larger classes or categories of vocabulary.

Follow-up and Enrichment Activities

Phonics
Teachers may find it opportune to help students with instruction in (or review of) phonics skills in conjunction with the *Spelling* exercise. Some students may find it difficult to isolate sounds in multisyllabic words.

Affixes
Teachers may wish to build on the *Word Families* exercise to have the students identify and discuss prefixes, suffixes, and common word endings found among the words under review.

Mastery Tests (Optional Purchase)
Once the work of the Review in the Student Text has been completed, the teacher may administer the corresponding *Mastery Test* in Cycle One or Two of the Supplementary Testing Program (see p. xiii below).

Final Mastery Test

The **Final Mastery Test** in the Student Text (student pages 140–143) is designed as a practice test of 50 items that gives students and teachers reasonably good insight into how much progress has been made during the year and what kind of additional work is in order.

The exercise types are for the most part the same as or similar to those in the Units and Reviews. The exception is **Part of Speech**, which occurs only in the Final Mastery Test. In this exercise students must identify the part of speech of a taught word as it is used in an illustrative phrase.

The purpose of the Final Mastery Test is threefold.

- It can serve as an informal evaluation of achievement to date;

- It can serve as a reinforcement activity;

- It can serve as a before-and-after comparison when used in conjunction with the Diagnostic Test.

For whichever purpose the test is used, it is both *a testing and a teaching device*, the culminating step in a process involving many class periods and therefore should be given careful attention.

SUPPLEMENTARY TESTING PROGRAM
(Optional Purchase)

The *Supplementary Testing Program* for Level Blue consists of two student Test Booklets (designated Cycle One and Cycle Two) designed to be used for varied and secure testing over a two-year period. It may be used purely as a testing program following the completion of work on the corresponding part or parts of the Student Text. Or it may be used for reteaching purposes. Or it may be tailored to serve some combination of purposes, depending upon the progress and achievement of a class or of individual students. The yearly and weekly plans given on pages xiv–xvii outline ways in which the Student Text and the Supplementary Testing Program might be used together to best advantage.

The Test Booklets are organized to mirror closely that of the Student Text. A 2-page Unit Test is provided for each of the 16 Units, a 2-page Mastery Test to correspond with each of the four Reviews, and a 4-page Final Mastery Test to supplement that in the Student Text. (There are no Cumulative Reviews in the Supplementary Testing Program.)

The Unit Test consists of 25 items; and the four sets of exercises in each (**Match the Meaning**, **Completing the Sentence**, **Synonyms**, and **Antonyms**) follow their counterparts in the Units and Reviews of the Student Text.

The Mastery Test is comprised of four sets of exercises as well. In **Word Meanings** students must match definitions with given words. The **Part of Speech** exercise is identical to that found in the Final Mastery Test of the Student Text. And in format and design the two sets of items in **Completing the Sentence** follow that of the Cumulative Reviews found in the Student Text.

In the Final Mastery Test are 50 consecutively numbered items, again including **Word Meanings**, **Completing the Sentence**, **Synonyms**, and **Antonyms**. Also included in the Final Mastery Test are a **Spelling** exercise and a **Word Associations** exercise patterned after those in the Student Text.

The answers to all of the items tested in the Supplementary Testing Program are given in the keys on pages xxv–xxxii of this Guide.

IMPLEMENTING THE PROGRAM

The format of the VOCABULARY WORKSHOP program allows for great flexibility. The teacher can easily adjust the activity assignments to conform to the special needs of an entire class, of groups within the class, or of individual students.

Schedule for the Year (25 Weeks)

The chart below shows how the various components of the VOCABULARY WORKSHOP program can be scheduled effectively over an academic year lasting 25 weeks. (The abbreviation STP C1/C2 stands for Supplementary Testing Program Cycle One or Two.)

Week	Student Text	Follow-Up Activities
1	Vocabulary of Vocabulary	
2	Diagnostic Test	
3	Unit 1	Creative Writing Unit Test 1 (STP C1/C2)
4	Unit 2	Creative Writing Unit Test 2 (STP C1/C2)
5	Unit 3	Creative Writing Unit Test 3 (STP C1/C2)
6	Unit 4	Creative Writing Unit Test 4 (STP C1/C2)
7	Review Units 1–4	Reviewing Phonics Mastery Test 1 (STP C1/C2)
8	Unit 5	Unit Test 5 (STP C1/C2) Creative Writing
9	Unit 6	Unit Test 6 (STP C1/C2) Creative Writing
10	Unit 7	Unit Test 7 (STP C1/C2) Creative Writing
11	Unit 8	Unit Test 8 (STP C1/C2) Creative Writing
12	Review Units 5–8	Mastery Test 2 (STP C1/C2) Reviewing Phonics
13	Cumulative Test 1–8	
14	Unit 9	Unit Test 9 (STP C1/C2) Creative Writing

Week	Student Text	Follow-Up Activities
15	Unit 10	Unit Test 10 (STP C1/C2) Creative Writing
16	Unit 11	Unit Test 11 (STP C1/C2) Creative Writing
17	Unit 12	Unit Test 12 (STP C1/C2) Creative Writing
18	Review Units 9–12	Mastery Test 3 (STP C1/C2) Reviewing Phonics
19	Unit 13	Unit Test 13 (STP C1/C2) Creative Writing
20	Unit 14	Unit Test 14 (STP C1/C2) Creative Writing
21	Unit 15	Unit Test 15 (STP C1/C2) Creative Writing
22	Unit 16	Unit Test 16 (STP C1/C2) Creative Writing
23	Review Units 13–16	Mastery Test 4 (STP C1/C2) Reviewing Phonics
24	Cumulative Review 9–16	Final Mastery Test (STP C1/C2)
25	Final Mastery Test	

The following notes should prove helpful when adapting the chart to individual needs:

• Though the chart shows a disposition of material over 25 weeks, the time period can be extended to as many as 31 weeks simply by increasing the time allotment for the items under weeks 7, 12, 18, 23, 24, and 25, to 2 weeks.

• It is *not* to be supposed that *every* item listed under Follow-Up Activities is meant to be covered during the week specified. The listings here are designed to offer teacher options from which to choose in order to tailor the VOCABULARY WORKSHOP program to the specific needs of a particular class. This is also true of the sections or subsections into which some of the Follow-Up components are divided.

• The average time allotment per class session is estimated to be about 20 minutes, but here again teachers will have to adapt this estimate to the needs of individual groups.

Weekly Schedules

There is no single formula or plan that will be sure to yield optimum results for the program. Experience will soon guide the teacher to modifications that are likely to work best under specific conditions.

Using the Units

Following are two plans for using the Units effectively on a weekly basis:

Weekly Plan for Using the Units

MODEL A — 3 Sessions (35–40 minutes)		
Day	**Classwork**	**Homework**
1	Present Definitions Present Pronunciation Write each word	Match the Meaning Synonyms/Antonyms
2	Completing the Sentence Word Associations	Correct previous homework Write sentences Test study
3	Unit Test (STP C1/C2)	Review corrected sentences

MODEL B — 5 Sessions (20 minutes)		
Day	**Classwork**	**Homework**
1	Present Definitions Present Pronunciation Review Unit Test	Match the Meaning Add illustrative sentences to Vocabulary Notebook
2	Review Match the Meaning Write each word	Synonyms/Antonyms
3	Review Synonyms/Antonyms Completing the Sentence	Word Associations Write sentences
4	Review Word Associations Review sentences	Test study
5	Unit Test (STP C1/C2)	Review corrected sentences

Using the Reviews

Following are two models for using the Reviews effectively on a weekly basis.

Weekly Plan for using the Reviews

MODEL A — 3 Sessions (35–40 minutes)		
Day	**Classwork**	**Homework**
1	Present: Selecting Word Meanings Spelling/Phonics* Antonyms Word Associations	Vocabulary in Context Analogies Phonics assignment*
2	Review homework Word Families Word Games Review phonics*	Test study
3	Mastery Test (STP C1/C2)	Remedial work as needed

MODEL B — 5 Sessions (20 minutes)		
Day	**Classwork**	**Homework**
1	Selecting Word Meanings Analogies	Spelling Word Families
2	Review Spelling/Phonics* Review Word Families	Antonyms Vocabulary in Context
3	Review Antonyms Review Vocabulary in Context	Word Games
4	Share Analogies Parts of Speech	Test study
5	Mastery Test (STP C1/C2)	

*See p. xii for reference to phonics skills

Using the Cumulative Reviews

Following are two models for using the Cumulative Reviews effectively on a weekly basis.

Weekly Plan for Using the Cumulative Reviews

MODEL A — 3 Sessions (35–40 minutes)		
Day	Classwork	Homework
1	Definitions Antonyms	Completing the Sentence
2	Review Completing the Sentence Classifying	Test study
3	Remediate as needed	

MODEL B — 5 Sessions (20 minutes)		
1	Definitions	Antonyms
2	Review Antonyms	Completing the Sentence
3	Review Completing the Sentence	Classifying
4	Review Classifying	Test study
5	Remediate as needed	

Implementing the Weekly Schedules

The following may prove helpful when adapting the foregoing schedules to specific situations.

• The models shown are, as their designation suggests, *purely models*—that is, starting points. Accordingly, the teacher is expected to adapt them to the particular situation at hand.

• Place assignments and timings are to some extent hypothetical. Teachers should switch items around and adjust timings as needed. Similarly, items may be modified or deleted and new items inserted as the teacher sees fit.

• Multiple listings in a Day's entry for either Classwork or Homework are to be seen as options from which the teacher should select appropriate material. It is unlikely that the teacher could cover all the suggested material in the indicated time allotment.

• With some adjustment, the allotments for each day can accommodate a 2- or 4-day arrangement. There is usually too much material to cover in 1 day, and a 1-day approach is, therefore, *not* suggested.

Alternative Approaches to Using the Program

Writing Approach

Research has shown that vocabulary acquisition is maximized when learning is authentically contextualized—when learners have a "real-life" purpose for acquiring and using a new word. Activities such as the following can provide these authentic contexts.

• Students can create *Vocabulary Journals* in which they use the key words to express experiences, thoughts, or feelings that are personally meaningful. They are free to keep these entries for their eyes only or to share them with others.

• Students can use the key words in personal letters to friends and relatives or in letters to the editor of the school or local newspaper. Students should write about subjects of real interest and concern to them.

• Students can use the key words to write descriptions of people they know or characters they are interested in. These character sketches or personality profiles may be written for a class yearbook, for a book report, or as a reference for a friend.

Literature-Based Approach

The VOCABULARY WORKSHOP program for Levels Blue and Orange can be combined with the titles listed below to form a *literature-based approach* to vocabulary study. Seeing the words they are studying in action in classic and contemporary literature will reinforce student appreciation of the value of possessing a good active-use vocabulary.

Literature to Use with the Program

Author	Title	Type
Avi	*Poppy*	Animal/Adventure
Babbit, Natalie	*The Search for Delicious*	Fantasy/Dictionary Definitions
Banks, Lynne Reid	*The Indian in the Cupboard*	Fantasy/Adventure
Brink, Carol Ryrie	*Caddie Woodlawn*	Historical/Prairie
Brittain, Bill	*The Wish Giver*	Mystery/Suspense
Burnford, Shirley	*The Incredible Journey*	Animal/Adventure
Byars, Betsy	*Summer of the Swans*	Realistic/Family
Clement, Andrew	*Frindle*	Realistic/History of Language
Conrad, Pam	*My Daniel*	Mystery/Historical Prairie
	Our House	Short Stories/Humor/Levittown
Curtis, Christopher Paul	*The Watsons Go to Birmingham–1963*	Historical/African American
Dorris, Michael	*Morning Girl*	Historical/Native American
Fitzgerald, John D.	*The Great Brain*	Realistic/Humor
Fitzhugh, Louise	*Harriet the Spy*	Realistic/Humor
Fleischman, Sid	*The Whipping Boy*	Fantasy/Adventure
Gardiner, John R.	*Stone Fox*	Adventure/Historical
George, Jean Craighead	*My Side of the Mountain*	Adventure/Survival

Author	Title	Type
Gipson, Frederick	*Old Yeller*	Animal/Realistic
Gray, Lulu	*Falcon's Egg*	Fantasy/Family
King-Smith, Dick	*Babe: The Gallant Pig*	Animal/Humor
	School Mouse	Animal/Books & Reading
Konigsburg, E.L.	*The View From Saturday*	Realistic/Language Contest
Lawson, Robert	*Ben and Me*	Historical/Franklin/Animal
Lofting, Hugh	*The Story of Doctor Doolittle*	Animal/Fantasy/Adventure
Lord, Betty Bao	*In the Year of the Boar and Jackie Robinson*	Historical/Chinese-American
Lowry, Lois	*Number the Stars*	Historical/WWII
MacLachlan, Patricia	*Sarah Plain and Tall*	Historical/Prairie
	The Facts and Fictions of Minna Pratt	Realistic/Musicians
McCloskey, Robert	*Homer Price*	Short Stories/Humor
Merrill, Jean	*The Pushcart War*	Realistic/Humor
Mohr, Nicholasa	*Felita*	Realistic/Hispanic
Mowat, Farley	*Owls in the Family*	Autobiography
Naylor, Phyllis Reynolds	*Shiloh*	Realistic/Animal
Noble, Sarah	*The Courage of Sarah Noble*	Autobiography/Westward Expansion
North, Sterling	*Rascal*	Autobiography/Animal/Humor
Norton, Mary	*The Borrowers*	Fantasy/Family
O'Brien, Robert	*Mrs. Frisby and the Rats of Nimh*	Animal/Fantasy
Paulson, Gary	*Hatchet*	Adventure/Survival
Sebestyn, Ouida	*Words by Heart*	Historical/African-American/ Bible Studies
Snyder, Zilpha Keatley	*Cat Running*	Historical/Great Depression/ Dust Bowl
Spinelli, Jerry	*Maniac Magee*	Realistic/Tall Tale
Steig, William	*Dominic*	Animal/Humor/Fantasy
Tate, Eleanor	*Thank You, Dr. Martin Luther King Jr.*	Historical/Realistic
Taylor, Mildred	*Mississippi Bridge*	Historical/African-American/ Prejudice
Taylor, Sidney	*All-of-a-Kind Family*	Historical Fiction/NYC/Jewish
Woodson, Jacqueline	*Last Summer with Maizon*	African-American/Friendship/ Realistic
Yep, Lawrence	*Dragonwings*	Historical/San Francisco Earthquake/Chinese-American

To coordinate reading and vocabulary study, the following may prove helpful:

- Suggest to the students that they copy into their Vocabulary Journals the taught words that they come across in their reading, and that they copy out, too, the sentence in which the word has been used, the author's name, and the title of the work.

Content-Area Approach

VOCABULARY WORKSHOP can be used to enhance student understanding and use of vocabulary in other areas of the curriculum such as social studies and history, science and health, consumer education and economics, by making use of the following strategies:

- Students, working in pairs or small groups, can choose sentence clusters from *Completing the Sentence* or *Vocabulary in Context* and discuss the larger context in which these sentences could have appeared, such as in a history or mathematics textbook, a daily newspaper, a book review, a personal letter, or a scientific article.

- Students can work together to link individual vocabulary words to a *particular content area*. Then working in pairs, they can find "real-world" examples of the words used in context in that content area.

Useful Classroom Techniques

Classroom experience and research have shown that some students learn more readily when they can exercise a great deal of personal choice and interact with others. VOCABULARY WORKSHOP can be adapted in the following ways to accommodate such students.

Cooperative Activities

Working cooperatively does not just mean working in proximity to other students or dividing an assignment or project into discrete tasks. Rather it means that students take individual and collective responsibility for the learning of all members of the group and for the successful completion of the group goal.

Oral and Kinesthetic Activities

- One student can write the taught words in a given Unit on the chalkboard while the rest of the class is divided into pairs or small groups. A member of each group will read a numbered item from the Unit aloud. The rest of the group will confer and then supply the required vocabulary word.

- Students can work together to create puns, riddles and rhymes using the words. They may want to collect and publish their creations in illustrated books.

- Members of a group can work together to improvise stories, skits, or pantomimes that illustrate the meanings of the words in a given Unit, while other group members guess the word being illustrated.

Written Activities

• Students can work together in pairs or small groups to create their own vocabulary lists, based on their reading in all areas of the curriculum and on their personal reading and writing.

• The class might as a whole make up a unit of their own, based upon the structure of the units in the Student Text. Students might be assigned to work in groups to develop each part of the unit.

• Students might create their own mini-dictionaries based on the word lists in VOCABULARY WORKSHOP and/or on categories or groups of words that are of particular importance or meaning to them.

Alternative Types of Assessment

The following types of assessment may be used in addition to or in lieu of the objective-scoring materials provided in the VOCABULARY WORKSHOP. The emphasis here is on monitoring understanding rather than on ranking students.

Self-Evaluation

Students can use their journals to reflect on their own process of learning and use of new words. They may consider, for example, which words from Level Blue of VOCABULARY WORKSHOP they understood quickly and used frequently and why.

Teacher-Student Conferencing

Meetings take place at every stage of the vocabulary-acquisition process. Meeting over time allows teachers to assess students' developing understanding of words as used in specific contexts.

Observation

Using a checklist of two or three important criteria, the teacher can observe and evaluate students while they are interacting in groups or engaging in other oral activities. Teachers can also probe for deeper levels of comprehension by asking students to clarify or give reasons for their choice of word or context.

Peer Evaluation

Students meet in pairs or small groups to develop standards to evaluate their vocabulary. They then apply their standards to their peers' oral or written expression, giving positive feedback and concrete suggestions for improvement.

Portfolio Assessment

By having students collect and save self-selected samples of their writing over a period of time, teachers have an ongoing record of students' vocabulary development and of their facility in using words in context.

Multimodal Assessment

Students with strong nonverbal competencies can be given the opportunity to demonstrate in nonverbal media their understanding of new vocabulary. For example, they can draw, paint, model, dance, compose music, or construct objects to communicate their comprehension of a word and its definition.

Teacher Resources

The following lists have been compiled to assist the teacher in the effective presentation of the VOCABULARY WORKSHOP program.

Dictionaries

Merriam Webster *Collegiate Dictionary* [Tenth Edition] (Springfield, MA: Merriam Webster, 1994)

Webster's Third New International Dictionary (Springfield, MA: G. & C. Merriam, 1971)

12,000 Words [A Supplement to Webster's Third International Dictionary] (Springfield, MA: Merriam Webster, 1986)

American Heritage Dictionary (Boston: Houghton Mifflin, 1982)

The Random House Dictionary of the English Language [Unabridged Edition] (NY: Random House, 1987)

Thesauri

Roget's II The New Thesaurus (Boston: Houghton Mifflin, 1988)

Chapman, R.L. (Ed.). *Roget A to Z* (NY: Harper Perennial, 1994)

Laird, C. *Webster's New World Thesaurus* (NY: Warner Books, 1990)

Random House Thesaurus (NY: Random House, 1984)

Rodale, J. [Revised by Urdang, L. and La Roche, N.] *The Synonym Finder* (Emmaus, PA: Rodale Press, 1978)

Urdang, L. *The Oxford Thesaurus* (NY: Oxford University Press, 1992)

Other Useful Resources

Bernstein, T. *Reverse Dictionary* (NY: Random House, 1988)

Bryson, B. *A Dictionary of Troublesome Words* (NY: Viking Penguin, 1988)

DeVries, M. *The Complete Word Book* (Englewood Cliffs, NJ: Prentice-Hall, 1991)

Dixson, R. *Essential Idioms in English* (Englewood Cliffs, NJ: Prentice ESL, 1987)

Evans, I. H. (Ed.) *Brewer's Dictionary of Phrase & Fable* (NY: Harper & Row, 1981)

Harrison, G. *Vocabulary Dynamics* (NY: Warner Books, 1992)

Lemay, H. et al. *The Facts on File Dictionary of New Words* (NY: Facts on File, 1989)

Morris, W. and M. Morris *Dictionary of Word & Phrase Origins* (NY: Harper & Row, 1981)

Orgel, J.R. *Building an Enriched Vocabulary* (NY: William H. Sadlier, Inc., 1995)

Paxson, W. *New American Dictionary of Confusing Words* (NY: NAL-Dutton, 1990)

Shipley, J. *Dictionary of Word Origins* (Glenville, IL: Greenwood Press, 1988)

Webster's Word Histories (Springfield, MA: Merriam Webster, 1989)

Computer Resources

GENERAL REFERENCE

American Heritage Electronic Dictionary III WordStar

Encarta: A Multimedia Encyclopedia Microsoft

WORD STUDY

Analogies Tutorial Hartley Courseware

IBM Vocabulary Series Level IV IBM Educational Systems

Lucky 7 Vocabulary Games—Intermediate Que

Testtaker's Edge with Words Que

Vocabulary Building II Resource Software

Vocabulary Building Skills IBM Educational Systems

Vocabulary Source Files—Junior High Microphys Programs

Word Knowledge Skills IBM Educational Systems

Answers to Challenge Exercises in Analogies Section of Reviews:

Review I, p. 39

Analogy:	**lamb** is to **sheep** as **calf** is to **cow**.
Relationship:	A lamb is a baby sheep; a calf is a baby cow.

Analogy:	**fragile** is to **break** as **flexible** is to **bend**.
Relationship:	Fragile things break easily; flexible things bend easily.

Review II, p. 69

Analogy:	**blunt** is to **keen** as **civilian** is to **soldier**.
Relationship:	Blunt and keen are opposites/antonyms; civilian and soldier are also opposites/antonyms.

Analogy:	**blemish** is to **flaw** as **barrier** is to **obstacle**.
Relationship:	Blemish and flaw are synonyms/mean the same; barrier and obstacle also are synonyms/mean the same.

Analogy:	**club** is to **blunt** as **sword** is to **keen**.
Relationship:	A club is a blunt weapon; a sword is a keen weapon.

Review III, p. 103

Analogy:	**apple** is to **fruit** as **carrot** is to **vegetable**.
Relationship:	An apple is a type of fruit; a carrot is a type of vegetable.

Analogy:	**wolf** is to **predator** as **sheep** is to **prey**.
Relationship:	A wolf is an example of a predator; a sheep is an example of prey.

Analogy:	**appeal** is to **attract** as **gauge** is to **measure**.
Relationship:	Appeal and attract are synonyms/mean the same; gauge and measure also are synonyms/mean the same.

Review IV, p. 133

Analogy:	**slaughter** is to **massacre** as **revolt** is to **mutiny**.
Relationship:	Slaughter and massacre are synonyms/mean the same; revolt and mutiny also are synonyms/mean the same.

Analogy:	**pencil** is to **write** as **fork** is to **eat**.
Relationship:	A pencil is used for writing; a knife is used for eating.

Analogy:	**positive** is to **negative** as **yes** is to **no**.
Relationship:	Positive and negative are opposites/antonyms; yes and no are also opposites/antonyms.

Analogy:	**positive** is to **yes** as **negative** is to **no**.
Relationship:	Yes is a positive; no is a negative.

Answer Key to Level Blue Supplementary Testing Program
Cycle One

UNIT 1
1. **c** temporary
2. **a** cancel
3. **d** solitary
4. **b** scuffle
5. **d** veteran
6. **d** reject
7. **c** document
8. blunder
9. continuous
10. fragile
11. reject
12. myth
13. distributed
14. **d** issue
15. **a** prove
16. **c** single
17. **b** error
18. **c** tale
19. **a** fight
20. **a** renew
21. **d** hardy
22. **b** rookie
23. **d** accept
24. **a** interrupted
25. **c** permanent

UNIT 2
1. **c** impressive
2. **a** strategy
3. **b** convert
4. **d** justify
5. **b** misleading
6. **a** assault
7. **d** Productive
8. dispute
9. villain
10. numerous
11. shrewd
12. abandoned
13. assault
14. **a** transformed
15. **b** sharp
16. **d** deceptive
17. **c** scheme
18. **b** striking
19. **a** defend

20. **b** defend
21. **a** idle
22. **d** agree
23. **a** occupy
24. **c** few
25. **b** hero

UNIT 3
1. **b** miniature
2. **d** postpone
3. **c** straggle
4. **a** consist
5. **d** obstacle
6. **d** haven
7. **c** bluff
8. monarch
9. cautious
10. treacherous
11. despised
12. vivid
13. bluff
14. **b** hurdles
15. **d** tiny
16. **a** delay
17. **a** wander
18. **d** hearty
19. **b** is made of
20. **a** daring
21. **b** trap
22. **d** faithful
23. **c** commoner
24. **b** adore
25. **d** dull

UNIT 4
1. **a** mishap
2. **d** aggressive
3. **b** hazy
4. **c** associate
5. **b** span
6. **a** linger
7. **d** Luxurious
8. glamour
9. deceive
10. flexible
11. emigrate
12. overwhelmed

13. linger
14. **a** bridge
15. **a** blunder
16. **d** relocate
17. **c** crush
18. **b** cheat
19. **d** beauty
20. **a** hurry
21. **d** timid
22. **b** rigid
23. **c** clear
24. **b** modest
25. **a** rival

MASTERY TEST I (UNITS 1–4)
1. mishap
2. deceive
3. impressive
4. scuffle
5. obstacle
6. V
7. N
8. A
9. A
10. V
11. V
12. N
13. V
14. N
15. A
16. postpone
17. abandon
18. luxurious
19. bluff
20. distribute
21. document
22. misleading
23. productive
24. emigrate
25. consist

UNIT 5
1. **d** Blunt
2. **a** fatigue
3. **c** blemish
4. **b** transport
5. **c** persecute
6. **d** Hospitality
7. **a** conclude
8. capable
9. festive

Cycle One

10. detect
11. nomads
12. supreme
13. concluded
14. **d** haul
15. **a** wanderers
16. **c** spot
17. **b** torment
18. **d** defect
19. **c** greatest
20. **a** tactful
21. **d** begin
22. **a** hostility
23. **c** gloomy
24. **d** unqualified
25. **c** energy

UNIT 6

1. **a** provoke
2. **d** duplicates
3. **b** conceal
4. **b** capacity
5. **c** spurt
6. **b** civilian
7. **a** apparent
8. vast
9. accomplish
10. keen
11. withdrew
12. undoing
13. capacity
14. **d** downfall
15. **a** gift
16. **d** surge
17. **b** acute
18. **c** subtract
19. **c** achieve
20. **a** military
21. **c** tiny
22. **b** reveal
23. **d** original
24. **b** uncertain
25. **c** calm

UNIT 7

1. **c** jolt
2. **b** shrivel
3. **a** Senseless

4. **d** considerable
5. **c** deputy
6. **b** Industrious
7. **d** compose
8. calculate
9. rejoice
10. barrier
11. reliable
12. loot
13. compose
14. **d** rattled
15. **a** assistant
16. **c** settle
17. **b** untiring
18. **b** determine
19. **b** booty
20. **b** opening
21. **d** mourn
22. **c** swelling
23. **b** smart
24. **a** slight
25. **d** fickle

UNIT 8

1. **c** Mature
2. **a** demolish
3. **b** observant
4. **d** alternate
5. **c** feat
6. **a** enforce
7. **d** Energetic
8. strive
9. resigned
10. demolish
11. hearty
12. verdict
13. primary
14. **c** achievement
15. **a** struggle
16. **b** leave
17. **b** replacement
18. **d** ruling
19. **c** destroy
20. **a** idle
21. **d** secondary
22. **b** phony
23. **c** disregard
24. **a** unripe
25. **d** inattentive

MASTERY TEST II (UNITS 5–8)

1. capacity
2. provoke
3. mature
4. blunt
5. deputy
6. A
7. N
8. A
9. V
10. N
11. N
12. V
13. A
14. N
15. V
16. undoing
17. calculate
18. fatigue
19. duplicate
20. shrivel
21. supreme
22. enforce
23. demolish
24. withdraw
25. jolt

UNIT 9

1. **a** considerate
2. **d** humiliated
3. **c** downfall
4. **b** displace
5. **c** vicinity
6. **a** Improper
7. **c** cherish
8. identical
9. polled
10. brisk
11. estimated
12. soothe
13. downfall
14. **b** survey
15. **d** neighborhood
16. **a** treasure
17. **c** guess
18. **b** unsuitable
19. **d** uproot
20. **c** different
21. **a** thoughtless
22. **b** praise
23. **d** worsen
24. **c** sluggish
25. **a** triumph

Cycle One

UNIT 10

1. **b** abolish
2. **d** Thrifty
3. **c** dictator
4. **d** visual
5. **a** famine
6. **b** prey
7. **c** condemn
8. expands
9. descend
10. appeal
11. portable
12. brittle
13. condemn
14. **d** tyrant
15. **b** victim
16. **a** ban
17. **d** come down
18. **a** plea
19. **d** seeing
20. **c** applaud
21. **d** bendable
22. **a** immovable
23. **b** extravagant
24. **a** reduce
25. **c** plenty

UNIT 11

1. **b** security
2. **c** avalanche
3. **d** navigate
4. **a** selective
5. **a** ensure
6. **d** absurd
7. **c** Reasonable
8. plea
9. tart
10. classify
11. principle
12. nestle
13. avalanche
14. **a** cascade
15. **d** standards
16. **b** steer
17. **c** appeal
18. **d** catalog
19. **b** snuggle
20. **d** impractical
21. **a** risk
22. **c** sweet
23. **b** careless
24. **a** peril
25. **a** sensible

UNIT 12

1. **a** Appliances
2. **d** daze
3. **b** Migrant
4. **c** rotate
5. **d** flimsy
6. **c** confirm
7. **b** presentable
8. abuse
9. neutral
10. shredded
11. gauge
12. pitiless
13. confirm
14. **a** assess
15. **c** stupor
16. **b** switch
17. **d** drifters
18. **c** check
19. **a** utensil
20. **b** shabby
21. **d** convincing
22. **c** opinionated
23. **a** merciful
24. **d** repair
25. **b** cherish

MASTERY TEST III (UNITS 9–12)

1. migrant
2. appliance
3. security
4. plea
5. brittle
6. V
7. N
8. A
9. N
10. V
11. V
12. N
13. V
14. V
15. A
16. improper
17. abolish
18. estimate
19. visual
20. pitiless
21. principle
22. downfall
23. selective
24. navigate
25. neutral

UNIT 13

1. **c** acquire
2. **a** sprawl
3. **b** widespread
4. **a** monotonous
5. **d** massacre
6. **c** latter
7. **b** exhibit
8. sanitary
9. exhibit
10. preserve
11. debate
12. foe
13. achievement
14. **d** slaughter
15. **a** lounge
16. **c** reveals
17. **b** clean
18. **d** sanctuary
19. **a** second
20. **c** failure
21. **b** comrade
22. **a** varied
23. **d** limited
24. **c** agreement
25. **b** lose

UNIT 14

1. **b** alibi
2. **a** discharge
3. **d** reign
4. **d** frank
5. **c** modify
6. **b** negative
7. **c** singular
8. confederate
9. swindle
10. pursue
11. economical
12. mutiny
13. negatives
14. **a** alter
15. **c** excuse

Cycle One

16. **d** cheat
17. **b** regime
18. **a** uprising
19. **d** chase
20. **c** hire
21. **d** plural
22. **a** favorable
23. **d** extravagant
24. **b** insincere
25. **c** enemy

UNIT 15

1. **d** complicate
2. **a** severe
3. **c** scorch
4. **b** trifle
5. **c** moral
6. **a** Courteous
7. **d** Universal
8. tragic
9. discomfort
10. eliminate
11. grieved
12. spectacle
13. universal
14. **d** blacken
15. **b** polite
16. **d** worldwide
17. **c** marvel
18. **b** remove
19. **a** trinket
20. **d** simplify
21. **b** wicked
22. **a** comical
23. **c** mild
24. **c** peace
25. **a** celebrate

UNIT 16

1. **d** assume
2. **b** rigid
3. **a** fertile
4. **a** mammoth
5. **c** peer
6. **d** rowdy
7. **b** endanger
8. safeguard
9. cram
10. fare

11. furnishes
12. trespassing
13. mammoth
14. **a** colleague
15. **c** threaten
16. **b** enormous
17. **d** suppose
18. **a** food
19. **d** intrude
20. **b** barren
21. **a** flexible
22. **d** threaten
23. **c** gentle
24. **a** withhold
25. **b** empty

MASTERY TEST IV (UNITS 13–16)

1. exhibit
2. sprawl
3. modify
4. assume
5. severe
6. V
7. N
8. A
9. A
10. N
11. V
12. N
13. V
14. N
15. A
16. negative
17. furnish
18. cram
19. sanitary
20. economical
21. preserve
22. complicate
23. safeguard
24. peer
25. eliminate

FINAL MASTERY TEST

1. hearty
2. pursue
3. universal
4. latter
5. aggressive
6. presentable
7. capable
8. rowdy
9. brittle

10. displace
11. fragile
12. no change: linger
13. alternate
14. soothe
15. absurd
16. achievement
17. singular
18. no change: fertile
19. abuse
20. keen
21. cherish
22. reign
23. flimsy
24. treacherous
25. prey
26. nestle
27. confirm
28. spectacle
29. **c** several
30. **a** obvious
31. **d** plead
32. **b** sensible
33. **a** obtain
34. **d** dreadful
35. **d** agreement
36. **a** fickle
37. **b** friend
38. **d** load
39. **a** climb
40. **b** impolite
41. **d**
42. **b**
43. **a**
44. **c**
45. **c**
46. **a**
47. **b**
48. **d**
49. **a**
50. **c**

Answer Key to Level Blue Supplementary Testing Program
Cycle Two

UNIT 1

1. **b** blunder
2. **a** distribute
3. **c** document
4. **c** myth
5. **d** Fragile
6. **b** continuous
7. **d** temporary
8. veteran
9. scuffle
10. solitary
11. documents
12. cancel
13. reject
14. **a** brawl
15. **b** divide
16. **a** dismiss
17. **c** legend
18. **d** expert
19. **c** certificate
20. **d** sociable
21. **d** interrupted
22. **a** permanent
23. **a** success
24. **c** sturdy
25. **b** continue

UNIT 2

1. **b** villain
2. **d** abandon
3. **a** misleading
4. **b** convert
5. **d** strategy
6. **a** shrewd
7. **d** productive
8. justify
9. villain
10. assault
11. dispute
12. numerous
13. impressive
14. **b** attack
15. **c** several
16. **a** awesome
17. **c** change
18. **d** explain
19. **c** scheme
20. **d** true
21. **a** inactive
22. **c** foolish
23. **b** occupy
24. **b** agree with
25. **c** heroine

UNIT 3

1. **d** miniature
2. **c** monarch
3. **a** consist
4. **c** straggle
5. **b** treacherous
6. **a** Cautious
7. **b** haven
8. bluff
9. despises
10. vivid
11. postponed
12. obstacles
13. straggled
14. **a** trick
15. **c** is made of
16. **d** lively
17. **b** dangerous
18. **d** careful
19. **b** roam
20. **d** trap
21. **a** move up
22. **a** enormous
23. **b** help
24. **b** commoner
25. **c** adore

UNIT 4

1. **c** span
2. **c** aggressive
3. **b** associate
4. **d** overwhelm
5. **a** hazy
6. **d** mishap
7. **b** deceive
8. emigrate
9. glamour
10. flexible
11. linger
12. luxurious
13. aggressive
14. **b** astound
15. **a** mistake
16. **b** charm
17. **d** relocate
18. **a** fool
19. **c** distance
20. **c** unbendable
21. **d** precise
22. **a** hurry
23. **b** simple
24. **c** timid
25. **c** foe

MASTERY TEST I (UNITS 1– 4)

1. misleading
2. luxurious
3. solitary
4. myth
5. postpone
6. A
7. V
8. A
9. A
10. N
11. N
12. A
13. V
14. N
15. V
16. strategy
17. shrewd
18. treacherous
19. consist
20. flexible
21. temporary
22. justify
23. impressive
24. linger
25. reject

Cycle Two

UNIT 5

1. **a** fatique
2. **d** blemish
3. **b** blunt
4. **c** persecute
5. **d** hospitality
6. **a** festive
7. **d** transport
8. hospitality
9. nomad
10. supreme
11. detect
12. conclude
13. capable
14. **c** carry
15. **d** find
16. **b** sleepiness
17. **b** wanderers
18. **c** greatest
19. **d** flaw
20. **c** gloomy
21. **a** unfit
22. **a** begin
23. **c** hostility
24. **c** tactful
25. **a** comfort

UNIT 6

1. **b** civilian
2. **a** provoke
3. **c** accomplish
4. **b** keen
5. **c** withdraw
6. **d** apparent
7. **a** undoing
8. spurt
9. vast
10. undoing
11. duplicate
12. capacity
13. concealed
14. **a** room
15. **a** complete
16. **d** obvious
17. **d** remove
18. **c** spacious
19. **a** surge
20. **b** reveal
21. **b** original
22. **a** dull

23. **d** success
24. **c** military
25. **d** calm

UNIT 7

1. **c** senseless
2. **a** calculate
3. **c** deputy
4. **b** jolt
5. **c** loot
6. **d** barrier
7. **b** reliable
8. shriveled
9. rejoice
10. jolt
11. Industrious
12. compose
13. considerable
14. **a** booty
15. **b** figure
16. **c** assistant
17. **a** lurch
18. **b** invent
19. **d** active
20. **c** small
21. **a** grieve
22. **d** clever
23. **c** fickle
24. **a** expand
25. **d** opening

UNIT 8

1. **a** resign
2. **b** alternate
3. **a** mature
4. **a** strive
5. **c** verdict
6. **d** demolish
7. **c** primary
8. energetic
9. strive
10. enforce
11. observant
12. feat
13. hearty
14. **c** rotate
15. **a** ruling
16. **b** quit
17. **c** attempt
18. **a** achievement

19. **c** main
20. **a** disregard
21. **a** build
22. **a** phony
23. **d** unripe
24. **c** careless
25. **a** lazy

MASTERY TEST II (UNITS 5–8)

1. conceal
2. spurt
3. compose
4. observant
5. blemish
6. V
7. V
8. A
9. N
10. A
11. A
12. V
13. A
14. N
15. N
16. senseless
17. reliable
18. energetic
19. resign
20. festive
21. provoke
22. vast
23. feat
24. mature
25. transport

UNIT 9

1. **d** vicinity
2. **b** poll
3. **c** estimate
4. **d** Brisk
5. **c** soothe
6. **d** cherish
7. **a** Improper
8. identical
9. considerate
10. vicinity
11. humiliated
12. downfall
13. displaced
14. **c** guess
15. **c** survey
16. **a** quiet
17. **c** fresh
18. **b** honor

Cycle Two

19. **a** neighborhood
20. **d** thoughtless
21. **c** settle
22. **b** praise
23. **a** polite
24. **c** different
25. **d** success

UNIT 10

1. **c** dictator
2. **b** thrifty
3. **c** visual
4. **a** expand
5. **c** appeal
6. **b** prey
7. **a** condemn
8. visual
9. Portable
10. descend
11. abolish
12. brittle
13. famine
14. **b** visible
15. **a** tyrant
16. **b** come down
17. **d** charm
18. **c** frugal
19. **a** feed
20. **d** immovable
21. **a** bendable
22. **a** praise
23. **b** reduce
24. **c** feast
25. **b** establish

UNIT 11

1. **d** avalanche
2. **a** nestle
3. **d** classify
4. **c** plea
5. **b** principles
6. **c** absurd
7. **d** realistic
8. ensure
9. navigate
10. security
11. selective
12. tart
13. avalanche
14. **b** catalog

15. **a** steer
16. **c** appeal
17. **a** standards
18. **d** snuggle
19. **b** landslide
20. **d** endanger
21. **a** gentle
22. **c** impractical
23. **c** careless
24. **d** danger
25. **b** sensible

UNIT 12

1. **b** rotate
2. **c** migrant
3. **a** appliance
4. **c** confirm
5. **b** daze
6. **c** flimsy
7. **a** abuse
8. gauge
9. neutral
10. pitiless
11. presentable
12. shred
13. rotates
14. **d** gadget
15. **a** trance
16. **d** assess
17. **c** drifters
18. **a** strip
19. **c** alternate
20. **b** care
21. **a** cancel
22. **c** opinionated
23. **b** kindhearted
24. **a** sturdy
25. **d** shabby

MASTERY TEST III (UNITS 9–12)

1. neutral
2. tart
3. senseless
4. condemn
5. cherish
6. V   11. V
7. V   12. V
8. A   13. A
9. N   14. A

10. N   15. N
16. considerate
17. descend
18. appeal
19. plea
20. shred
21. brisk
22. humiliate
23. dictator
24. avalanche
25. confirm

UNIT 13

1. **b** massacre
2. **a** sprawl
3. **a** achievement
4. **c** widespread
5. **d** acquire
6. **c** sanitary
7. **b** debate
8. preserve
9. sprawl
10. exhibit
11. monotonous
12. foe
13. latter
14. **d** far-reaching
15. **c** slaughter
16. **b** clean
17. **a** triumphs
18. **b** lounge
19. **c** refuge
20. **c** agree
21. **a** hide
22. **c** lively
23. **b** first
24. **a** friend
25. **d** lose

UNIT 14

1. **c** modify
2. **b** alibi
3. **d** reign
4. **b** swindle
5. **c** economical
6. **a** pursue
7. **d** singular
8. Confederate
9. negative

Cycle Two

10. swindle
11. mutiny
12. discharged
13. frank
14. **d** rule
15. **a** cheat
16. **c** excuse
17. **a** revise
18. **d** ally
19. **c** unusual
20. **b** flee
21. **a** appoint
22. **d** insincere
23. **c** wasteful
24. **d** positive
25. **a** obey

UNIT 15

1. **c** spectacle
2. **d** scorch
3. **c** universal
4. **b** complicate
5. **a** trifle
6. **b** Severe
7. **c** discomfort
8. courteous
9. tragic
10. eliminate
11. moral
12. grieve
13. spectacles
14. **b** general
15. **c** singe
16. **d** stern
17. **a** disastrous
18. **b** knickknacks
19. **c** show
20. **d** rude
21. **b** preserve
22. **a** peace
23. **b** rejoice
24. **d** wicked
25. **b** simplify

UNIT 16

1. **b** fare
2. **a** Peer
3. **b** trespass
4. **d** rowdy
5. **c** safeguard

6. **a** assume
7. **d** rigid
8. mammoth
9. cram
10. furnishes
11. endangers
12. fertile
13. trespass
14. **c** intrude
15. **b** food
16. **b** colleagues
17. **c** accept
18. **a** protect
19. **b** stuff
20. **a** protect
21. **c** barren
22. **d** small
23. **b** take
24. **a** flexible
25. **c** quiet

MASTERY TEST IV (UNITS 13–16)

1. acquire
2. widespread
3. cram
4. grieve
5. frank
6. V
7. V
8. A
9. A
10. A
11. N
12. N
13. V
14. N
15. V
16. assume
17. rigid
18. moral
19. achievement
20. modify
21. singular
22. swindle
23. discomfort
24. fertile
25. massive

FINAL MASTERY TEST

1. detect
2. dispute
3. miniature
4. mishap

5. abandon
6. withdraw
7. vicinity
8. portable
9. selective
10. migrant
11. endanger
12. trespass
13. no change : universal
14. trifle
15. pursue
16. no change : economical
17. monotonous
18. sprawl
19. rotate
20. appliance
21. considerable
22. hearty
23. navigate
24. estimate
25. overwhelm
26. capable
27. demolish
28. misleading
29. **b** complete
30. **c** jerk
31. **d** breakable
32. **a** comfort
33. **d** lone
34. **a** hurdle
35. **c** barren
36. **d** celebrate
37. **d** appoint
38. **c** defeat
39. **a** deny
40. **b** sweet
41. **b**
42. **d**
43. **d**
44. **a**
45. **c**
46. **b**
47. **a**
48. **c**
49. **a**
50. **c**

VOCABULARY WORKSHOP

LEVEL BLUE

Jerome Shostak

Sadlier-Oxford
A Division of William H. Sadlier, Inc.
New York, NY 10005-1002

VOCABULARY WORKSHOP

The classic program for:

- developing and enriching vocabulary resources
- promoting more effective communication in today's world
- improving vocabulary skills assessed on standardized tests

Acknowledgments

Christie's Images: 13.

Corbis: 19; UPI/Bettman: 49, 61; Hulton Deutsch Collection: 95.

H. Armstrong Roberts: 31, 83.

Tony Stone Images/ Hulton Getty Images: 25; Lorne Resnick: 43; Michael Busselle: 55; Lorentz Gullachsen: 77; Bruce Foster: 89; Michael Rosenfeld: 107; Mark Segal: 119; Gary Holscher: 125.

Illustrator

Daryl Stevens: 41, 71, 105, 135.

Request for permission to make copies of any part of this work should be mailed to:

Permissions Department
William H. Sadlier, Inc.
9 Pine Street
New York, NY 10005-1002

𝕊 is a registered trademark of William H. Sadlier, Inc.

Printed in the United States of America

ISBN: 0-8215-0405-3

3456789/01 00 99

CONTENTS

FOREWORD

For nearly half a century Vocabulary Workshop has proven a highly successful tool for promoting and guiding systematic vocabulary growth. Level Blue, one of two new additions to the Vocabulary Workshop series, is meant both to help younger students *increase* their vocabulary and *improve* their vocabulary skills. It has also been designed to help prepare students for vocabulary-related items found in standardized tests.

Mastery of the words introduced in this text will make students better readers and better writers—better readers because they will be able to understand and appreciate more of what they read, and better writers because they will have at hand a greater pool of words with which to express themselves. Many of the words introduced in this book are ones that students will encounter in social studies, science, and literature, as well as in their reading outside the classroom.

Word List	Level Blue contains 192 basic words selected on the basis of currency in present-day usage, frequency in recognized vocabulary lists and on standardized tests, and the latest grade-placement research.
Units	The words are grouped in 16 short, stimulating units that include: definitions (with pronunciation and parts of speech), reinforcement of meanings, synonyms and antonyms, in-context sentence completions, and word-association exercises.
Reviews	Four Reviews (one for every four units) reinforce the work of the units with challenging exercises that include analogies, vocabulary-in-context, and word games.
	Two Cumulative Reviews, the first covering the first 8 units, the second covering the last 8 units, provide further reinforcement.
Assessment	The Diagnostic Test provides ready assessment of student needs and preparedness at the outset of the term.
	The Final Mastery Test provides end-of-term assessment of student achievement.
Teacher Materials	A Teacher's Annotated Edition supplies answers to all of the exercises in the pupil text and an introduction to the Vocabulary Workshop program.
	The Supplementary Testing Program provides separate testing exercises covering the material found in the pupil text. Answers are in the Annotated Teacher's Edition.

THE VOCABULARY OF VOCABULARY

English has a large group of special terms to describe how words are used and how they are related to one another. These terms make up what we might call the "vocabulary of vocabulary." Learning to understand and use the vocabulary of vocabulary will help you to get better results in your vocabulary-building program.

Part of Speech

Every word in English plays some role in the language. What that role is determines how a word is classified grammatically. These classifications are called "parts of speech." In English there are eight parts of speech: nouns, pronouns, verbs, adjectives, adverbs, prepositions, conjunctions, and interjections. All of the words introduced in this book are nouns (abbreviated *n.*), verbs (*v.*), or adjectives (*adj.*).

A **noun** names a person, place, or thing. *Uncle, home,* and *food* are nouns. So are *Lincoln, Chicago,* and *Superbowl.* Nouns also name things such as ideas and feelings; for example, *justice, space,* and *anger* are nouns.

Verbs express action or a state of being. *Go, be, live, tell, write, speak, listen, leave, arrive,* and *behave* are verbs.

Adjectives describe or give information about nouns or other adjectives. *Happy, sad, quick, slow, big, little, black, white, first,* and *last* are adjectives.

Many English words act as more than one part of speech. The word *bend,* for example, can be a verb or a noun. Its part of speech depends upon the way it is used.

NOUN: We came to a bend in the river. [*bend* names a thing]

VERB: The wind made the trees bend. [*bend* expresses an action]

EXERCISES   For each sentence, circle the choice that identifies the part of speech of the word in **boldface**.

1. My brother is a **fast** runner.
   a. noun   b. verb   (c.) adjective

2. Let's **work** together to solve the problem.
   a. noun   (b.) verb   c. adjective

3. I have a lot of **work** to do this weekend.
   (a.) noun   b. verb   c. adjective

4. I'm wearing a **new** pair of socks.
   a. noun   b. verb   (c.) adjective

5. There were a lot of happy **faces** in the crowd.
   (a.) noun   b. verb   c. adjective

6. The front of the house **faces** East.
   a. noun   (b.) verb   c. adjective

Synonyms and Antonyms

Synonyms

A **synonym** is a word that means *the same* or *nearly the same* as another word.

EXAMPLES   gift — present   smart — clever

cry — weep   joy — happiness

thin — skinny   begin — start

EXERCISES   For each of the following groups circle the choice that is most nearly the **same** in meaning as the word in **boldface**.

1. **silent**	2. **jog**	3. **law**	4. **tidy**
a. noisy	a. crawl	(a.) rule	a. messy
b. kind	(b.) trot	b. school	b. small
c. playful	c. laugh	c. jail	c. new
(d.) quiet	d. stop	d. sheriff	(d.) neat

Antonyms

An **antonym** is a word that is *opposite* or *nearly opposite* in meaning to another word.

EXAMPLES   grow — shrink   huge — tiny

crowded — empty   victory — defeat

friend — enemy   hide — show

EXERCISES   For each of the following groups circle the choice that is most nearly **opposite** in meaning to the word in **boldface**.

1. **simple**	2. **wealth**	3. **punish**	4. **healthy**
a. easy	a. fame	(a.) reward	a. bossy
(b.) difficult	b. success	b. trust	b. messy
c. cheap	(c.) poverty	c. trick	c. sturdy
d. boring	d. taxes	d. remember	(d.) sickly

Context Clues

When you turn to the "Completing the Sentence" and "Vocabulary in Context" exercises in this book, look for clues built into the passages to guide you to the correct answers. There are three basic types of clues.

Restatement Clues   A restatement clue gives a *definition of,* or a *synonym for,* a missing word.

EXAMPLE   The climbers slowly made their way to the top of the mountain until at last they reached its very _____.

a. bottom   b. slope   c.)peak   d. range

Contrast Clues   A contrast clue gives an *antonym for,* or a phrase meaning *the opposite of,* a missing word.

EXAMPLE   The weather was mild at the foot of the mountain, but the conditions at the top were _____.

a. nice   b.)harsh   c. friendly   d. dry

Situational Clues   Sometimes the situation itself, as it is outlined in the sentence or passage, suggests the word that is missing but does not state the meaning directly.

EXAMPLE   After the long and dangerous return from the top of the mountain, the climbers were very _____.

a. bored   b.)weary   c. fresh   d. guilty

To figure out which word is missing from the sentence, ask yourself this question: How would the climbers feel after a "long and dangerous" journey? Would they feel bored? weary? fresh? guilty?

EXERCISES   Use context clues to choose the word that best completes each of the following sentences.

1. Why argue over such silly matters when we have so many _____ problems to deal with?

a. little   b. foolish   c.)serious   d. unimportant

2. We will have to _____ for hours to get rid of all the grime.

a. play   b. read   c. walk   d.)scrub

3. The noise in the crowded gym was so great that we could barely make ourselves heard above the _____.

a.)racket   b. score   c. chairs   d. referees

Analogies

An **analogy** is a comparison. For example, we can make an analogy, or comparison, between a computer and a human brain.

In this book and in many standardized tests you will be asked to find the relationship between two words. Then, to show that you understand that relationship, you will be asked to choose another pair of words that show the same relationship.

EXAMPLES

1. **close** is to **open** as

   a. dance is to swim

   b. hold is to pinch

   c. stop is to go

   d. talk is to chat

2. **push** is to **shove** as

   a. grab is to release

   b. giggle is to laugh

   c. hope is to try

   d. watch is to listen

In the first example, note that *close* and *open* are **antonyms**; they are opposite in meaning. Of the four choices given, which pair is made up of words that are also antonyms, or opposite in meaning? The answer, of course, is *c, stop is to go.*

In the second example, note that *push* and *shove* are **synonyms**; they have nearly the same meaning. Of the four choices given, which pair is made up of words that are also synonyms, or nearly the same in meaning? The answer is *b, giggle is to laugh.*

There are many other kinds of analogies besides ones based on synonyms and antonyms. For each of the exercises that follow, first study carefully the pair of words in **boldface**. Then, when you have figured out the relationship between the two words, look for another pair that has the same relationship. Circle the item that best completes the analogy, and then write the relationship on the lines provided.

3. **steel** is to **metal** as

   a. oak is to wood

   b. pencil is to pen

   c. glass is to bottle

   d. jewel is to diamond

Relationship: Steel is a type of metal; oak is a type of wood.

4. **page** is to **book** as

   a. baseball is to hockey

   b. cover is to magazine

   c. letter is to note

   d. leaf is to tree

Relationship: A book is made up of pages; a tree is made up of leaves.

5. **kitten** is to **cat** as

   a. chick is to egg

   b. horse is to colt

   c. puppy is to dog

   d. cub is to den

Relationship: A kitten is a baby cat; a puppy is a baby dog.

Pronunciation Key

The pronunciation is given for every basic word introduced in this book. The symbols, which are shown below, are similar to those that appear in most standard dictionaries. The author has consulted a large number of dictionaries for this purpose but has relied primarily on *Webster's Third New International Dictionary* and *The Random House Dictionary of the English Language (Unabridged)*.

Of course, there are many English words, including some that appear in this book, for which two (or more) pronunciations are commonly accepted. In virtually all cases where such words occur in this book, just one pronunciation is given. Exceptions to this rule are made, however, in cases when the pronunciation of a word changes according to its part of speech. For example, as a noun the word *object* is pronounced **'äb jekt**; as a verb it is pronounced **əb 'jekt**. These relatively simple pronunciation guides should be readily usable by students. It should be emphasized, however, that the best way to learn the pronunciation of a word is to listen to and imitate an educated speaker.

Vowels	ā	l*a*ke	e	str*e*ss	ü	b*oo*t, n*ew*
	a	m*a*t	ī	kn*i*fe	u̇	f*oo*t, p*u*ll
	â	c*a*re	i	s*i*t	ə	r*u*g, brok*e*n
	ä	b*a*rk, b*o*ttle	ō	fl*o*w	ər	b*ir*d, bett*er*
	au̇	d*ou*bt	ô	*a*ll, c*o*rd		
	ē	b*ea*t, word*y*	oi	*oi*l		

Consonants	ch	*ch*ild, le*c*ture	s	*c*ellar	wh	*wh*at
	g	*g*ive	sh	*sh*un	y	*y*ell
	j	*g*entle, bri*dge*	th	*th*ank	z	i*s*
	ŋ	si*ng*	t̶h̶	*th*ose	zh	mea*s*ure

All other consonants are sounded as in the alphabet.

Stress	The accent mark *precedes* the syllable receiving the major stress: en 'rich

Diagnostic Test

*For each of the following items circle the letter for the word or phrase that best expresses the meaning of the word in **boldface** in the introductory phrase.*

Example

a **frisky** puppy

a. wet   (b.) playful   c. sick   d. little

---

1. a **fragile** set of crystal glasses
   a. shiny   b. beautiful   c. matched   (d.) delicate

2. read about the **dispute**
   a. agreement   (b.) argument   c. election   d. discovery

3. **bluffed** a throw to first base
   a. caught   b. dropped   c. blocked   (d.) faked

4. painted in **vivid** colors
   (a.) brilliant   b. matching   c. contrasting   d. dull

5. a **span** of ninety feet
   a. ditch   (b.) length   c. road   d. depth

6. **lingered** at a party
   a. left   b. entertained   c. danced   (d.) stayed

7. lived like **nomads**
   a. athletes   (b.) wanderers   c. criminals   d. farmers

8. a **festive** mood
   a. sad   b. angry   c. generous   (d.) happy

9. a **keen** mind
   a. silly   b. troubled   (c.) sharp   d. dull

10. **composed** beautiful songs
    a. sang   (b.) wrote   c. played   d. listened to

11. a very **reliable** mechanic
    (a.) trustworthy   b. skilled   c. talkative   d. cheerful

12. wrote about her **feats**

    a. poems   b. relatives   (c.) deeds   d. shoes

13. the **primary** reason

    a. only   (b.) main   c. secret   d. wrong

14. **cherish** your friends

    a. argue with   b. forget   c. visit   (d.) treasure

15. made an **improper** turn

    (a.) wrong   b. left   c. unnecessary   d. sudden

16. survived a **famine**

    a. lack of shelter   (b.) lack of food   c. lack of news   d. lack of taste

17. **appealed** for volunteers

    a. voted   b. telephoned   (c.) asked   d. paid

18. an important **principle**

    a. act   b. goal   c. teacher   (d.) rule

19. a totally **absurd** idea

    a. interesting   (b.) foolish   c. sensible   d. confusing

20. **shreds** of paper

    (a.) bits   b. piles   c. pads   d. boxes

21. a **pitiless** dictator

    a. friendless   b. powerful   c. cheerful   (d.) heartless

22. surrounded by many **foes**

    a. deer   b. friends   (c.) enemies   d. neighbors

23. **pursued** the runaway horse

    (a.) chased   b. rode   c. saddled   d. fed

24. a **universal** problem

    (a.) worldwide   b. local   c. recent   d. temporary

25. enjoyed special holiday **fare**

    a. prayers   b. games   c. music   (d.) food and drink

Definitions

Study the spelling, pronunciation, part of speech, and definition given for each of the words below. Write the word in the blank space in the sentence that follows. Then read the synonyms and antonyms.

1. **blunder**
('blən dər)

(v.) to make a foolish or careless mistake; to move clumsily and carelessly
The hikers saw a bear _____ blunder _____ through the woods.
(n.) a serious or thoughtless mistake
I was terribly embarrassed by my _____ blunder _____.
SYNONYMS: to err, foul up, bungle, goof; an error, blooper
ANTONYMS: to triumph, succeed; a success, hit

2. **cancel**
('kan səl)

(v.) to call off or do away with; to cross out with lines or other marks to show that something cannot be used again
Maybe the principal will _____ cancel _____ classes if it continues to snow.
SYNONYMS: to stop, discontinue, drop, repeal, revoke
ANTONYMS: to renew, continue, extend, maintain

3. **continuous**
(kən 'tin yü əs)

(adj.) going on without a stop or break
_____ Continuous _____ TV coverage began shortly after news of the disaster broke.
SYNONYMS: ongoing, endless, ceaseless, unbroken, constant, perpetual
ANTONYMS: broken, discontinuous, interrupted

4. **distribute**
(di 'stri byüt)

(v.) to give out in shares; to scatter or spread
Our class will _____ distribute _____ leaflets announcing the school's fund-raising drive.
SYNONYMS: to divide, share, deal, issue
ANTONYMS: to gather, collect, hold

5. **document**
('dä kyə ment)

(n.) a written or printed record that gives information or proof
The librarian found the old _____ document _____ between the pages of a book.
(v.) to give written or printed proof; to support with evidence
Writers often _____ document _____ their sources.
SYNONYMS: a certificate, deed; to prove, support, establish

6. **fragile**
('fra jəl)

(adj.) easily broken or damaged, requiring special handling or care
The _____ fragile _____ antique was carefully packed to protect it during shipment.
SYNONYMS: weak, frail, breakable, delicate, brittle, flimsy
ANTONYMS: sturdy, hardy, strong, rugged, tough

The Greek god Zeus, shown here in a Roman sculpture, is the subject of many ancient **myths** (word 7).

7. **myth**
   (mith)

(n.) an old story that explains why something is or how it came to be; something imaginary

The play is based on an ancient Greek _____myth_____.

SYNONYMS: a legend, fable, tale, fantasy, fairy tale
ANTONYM: a fact

8. **reject**
   (ri 'jekt)

(v.) to refuse to accept, agree to, believe, or use

Why did you _____reject_____ the offer?

SYNONYMS: to deny, discard, junk, scrap, decline, dismiss
ANTONYMS: to take, accept, receive, welcome

9. **scuffle**
   ('skə fəl)

(v.) to fight or struggle closely with

A witness saw the two men _____scuffle_____ in an alley.

(n.) fight or struggle

Police officers were called in and broke up the _____scuffle_____.

SYNONYMS: to tussle, roughhouse, battle, brawl; a fistfight, clash

10. **solitary**
    ('sä lə ter ē)

(adj.) living or being alone; being the only one

The old man led a _____solitary_____ life.

SYNONYMS: single, one, only, sole, lone
ANTONYMS: sociable; several, many, numerous

11. **temporary**
    ('tem pə rer ē)

(adj.) lasting or used for a limited time

A blow to the head can cause a _____temporary_____ loss of memory.

SYNONYMS: short-term, passing, brief, momentary
ANTONYMS: lasting, long-lived, permanent

12. **veteran**
    ('ve tə rən)

(n.) a person who has served in the armed forces; a person who has a lot of experience

The President spoke to a group of _____veterans_____.

(adj.) having much experience in some job or field, seasoned

In her next movie, the actress will play a _____veteran_____ reporter.

SYNONYMS: expert, professional, experienced, skilled, accomplished
ANTONYMS: a beginner, newcomer, novice, rookie

13

For each item below choose the word whose meaning is suggested by the clue given. Then write the word in the space provided.

1. A roommate you have for only a month is a _____temporary_____ one.
   a. continuous   b. temporary   c. fragile   d. solitary

2. A black eye might be the result of a _____scuffle_____.
   a. scuffle   b. myth   c. veteran   d. blunder

3. To _____document_____ your age you might show a birth certificate or a driver's license.
   a. distribute   b. document   c. cancel   d. reject

4. A person who lives alone in the woods might be described as _____solitary_____.
   a. continuous   b. solitary   c. temporary   d. fragile

5. The "creation" stories of the Native Americans are examples of _____myths_____.
   a. blunders   b. documents   c. scuffles   d. myths

6. If I make a serious mistake, I commit a _____blunder_____.
   a. scuffle   b. document   c. myth   d. blunder

7. A box containing an item that can be broken easily might be stamped "_____fragile_____."
   a. solitary   b. temporary   c. fragile   d. continuous

8. A charity might _____distribute_____ food to the homeless.
   a. reject   b. cancel   c. scuffle   d. distribute

9. Something that goes on without stopping is _____continuous_____.
   a. continuous   b. temporary   c. solitary   d. fragile

10. To refuse a gift is to _____reject_____ it.
    a. cancel   b. scuffle   c. distribute   d. reject

11. A person who has a lot of experience at something is a _____veteran_____.
    a. blunder   b. myth   c. document   d. veteran

12. If I call off a party, I _____cancel_____ it.
    a. reject   b. blunder   c. cancel   d. scuffle

Synonyms

*For each item below choose the word that is most nearly the **same** in meaning as the word or phrase in **boldface**. Then write your choice on the line provided.*

1. a **constant** flow of traffic
   a. fragile   b. temporary   c. continuous   d. veteran   _continuous_

2. tried to hide the **blooper**
   a. document   b. myth   c. blunder   d. scuffle   _blunder_

3. not a **single** cent
   a. temporary   b. fragile   c. solitary   d. veteran   _solitary_

4. witnessed the **fight**
   a. myth   b. blunder   c. document   d. scuffle   _scuffle_

5. very important **records**
   a. veterans   b. documents   c. myths   d. blunders   _documents_

6. a collection of ancient **stories**
   a. documents   b. myths   c. veterans   d. blunders   _myths_

Antonyms

*For each item below choose the word that is most nearly **opposite** in meaning to the word or phrase in **boldface**. Then write your choice on the line provided.*

1. **renew** my subscription
   a. cancel   b. blunder   c. scuffle   d. distribute   _cancel_

2. **accept** the marriage proposal
   a. scuffle   b. reject   c. blunder   d. distribute   _reject_

3. a **novice** mountain climber
   a. temporary   b. fragile   c. continuous   d. veteran   _veteran_

4. **gather** the homework sheets
   a. reject   b. document   c. distribute   d. cancel   _distribute_

5. a **sturdy** device
   a. temporary   b. solitary   c. veteran   d. fragile   _fragile_

6. a **permanent** filling
   a. veteran   b. continuous   c. temporary   d. solitary   _temporary_

From the list of words on pages 12–13 choose the one that best completes each item below. Then write the word in the space provided. (You may have to change the word's ending.)

A VISIT TO A MUSEUM

■ Our class visited the museum on the last day of a(n) _____temporary_____ exhibit of ancient Greek vases. The vases had been on display for three months and were going to be returned to the European museums that had lent them.

■ Some of the vases were more than 2,000 years old. Because they were so old and _____fragile_____, we weren't allowed to touch them.

■ Security guards kept visitors a few feet from the display cases, so there was no chance that someone could _____blunder_____ into them.

■ The guide told us that the pictures painted on some of the vases were not of real people but characters from legends and _____myths_____.

■ One picture showed a(n) _____solitary_____ warrior fighting off a band of attackers. Our guide explained that the lone fighter was the Greek warrior Achilles and that his attackers were soldiers of Troy.

A FAMOUS DECLARATION

■ In refusing to accept English rule, the writers of the Declaration of Independence _____rejected_____ the claim that Parliament had sovereignty, or lawful power, over the American colonies.

■ Friends to the cause of American independence quickly printed and _____distributed_____ copies of the Declaration throughout the thirteen colonies.

■ The original _____document_____, one of America's historic treasures, is now on view at the National Archives building in Washington, D.C.

ON THE SOCCER FIELD

■ Two days of _____continuous_____ rain had turned the soccer field into a sea of mud and threatened to spoil the opening game of the season.

■ Before the game began, a _____scuffle_____ broke out in the stands when a few home-team fans came to blows with those rooting for the visiting team.

■ The referee threatened to _____cancel_____ the game and send all of the fans home if order were not restored.

■ Only when a handful of popular _____veterans_____ from both teams asked the fans to behave themselves did they finally settle down and let the game get underway.

*Circle the letter next to the word or expression that best completes the sentence or answers the question. Pay special attention to the word in **boldface.***

1. A person might emerge from a **scuffle**
   a. with spaghetti and meatballs
   b. with scrapes and bruises
   c. with dollars and cents
   d. with hugs and kisses

2. Someone who has **blundered** would
   a. feel embarrassed
   b. be confident
   c. feel proud
   d. be rewarded

3. A **solitary** tree would probably
   a. have needles
   b. be chopped down
   c. change color in the fall
   d. stand alone

4. A **continuous** loud noise might
   a. be hard to hear
   b. stop and start
   c. be soothing
   d. be annoying

5. Which of the following is a **document**?
   a. an old friend
   b. a telephone call
   c. a marriage license
   d. a good meal

6. If I **cancel** my piano lesson,
   a. I don't go
   b. I play very well
   c. I repair the piano
   d. I arrive late

7. A **temporary** problem is one that
   a. lasts a long time
   b. goes away
   c. no one can solve
   d. anyone can solve

8. In a **veteran's** closet you might find
   a. a skateboard
   b. a party dress
   c. a box of marbles
   d. an old uniform

9. When a teacher **distributes** a test
   a. he or she grades it
   b. he or she loses it
   c. he or she passes it out
   d. he or she collects it

10. Which of the following is usually **fragile**?
    a. a hammer
    b. a pair of scissors
    c. a light bulb
    d. a padlock

11. Someone who has been **rejected**
    a. might feel hurt
    b. might feel happy
    c. might get lost
    d. might get a cold

12. Which is a creature of **myth**?
    a. a rabbit
    b. a giraffe
    c. a duck
    d. a dragon

Definitions

Study the spelling, pronunciation, part of speech, and definition given for each of the words below. Write the word in the blank space in the sentence that follows. Then read the synonyms and antonyms.

1. **abandon**
   (ə 'ban dən)

   (v.) to give up on completely; to leave with no intention of returning
   The captain gave the order to _____ **abandon** _____ *ship.*

   SYNONYMS: to desert, forsake, cease, surrender
   ANTONYMS: to continue, stay, remain, occupy

2. **assault**
   (ə 'sôlt)

   (n.) a violent attack
   The victim was seriously injured in the _____ **assault** _____ .

   (v.) to attack violently or suddenly
   Dad dared us to _____ **assault** _____ *his snow fort.*

   SYNONYMS: invasion, raid, mugging, beating; to besiege, storm, attack
   ANTONYMS: to protect, defend, resist

3. **convert**
   (v., kən 'vərt;
   n., 'kän vərt)

   (v.) to change from one form to another
   A drop in temperature to 32° F will _____ **convert** _____ *water to ice.*

   (n.) a person who has changed from one opinion, belief, or religion to another
   The new _____ **convert** _____ *was introduced to the congregation.*

   SYNONYMS: to change, transform, turn, alter, switch
   ANTONYMS: to maintain, conserve, remain

4. **dispute**
   (di 'spyüt)

   (v.) to argue, debate, quarrel over; to question or doubt the truth of
   The committee members did not _____ **dispute** _____ *the merits of the bill.*

   (n.) an argument, quarrel, debate
   Why not try to resolve the _____ **dispute** _____ *peacefully?*

   SYNONYMS: to differ, disagree, contest, challenge; a conflict, disagreement, controversy
   ANTONYMS: to agree, harmonize; an agreement, understanding, accord

5. **impressive**
   (im 'pre siv)

   (adj.) having a strong effect, commanding attention
   The skater gave an _____ **impressive** _____ *performance.*

   SYNONYMS: memorable, striking, stirring, thrilling, awesome, splendid
   ANTONYMS: inferior, mediocre

6. **justify**
   ('jəs tə fī)

   (v.) to show to be fair or right; to give good reasons for
   Be prepared to _____ **justify** _____ *your behavior.*

   SYNONYMS: to defend, explain, support, excuse
   ANTONYMS: to convict, blame, accuse

In old movies the **villain** (word 12) often wore a black hat.

7. **misleading**
   (mis 'lē diŋ)

   (adj.) tending to give a wrong idea, often on purpose
   The lawyer called the statement _____misleading_____.
   SYNONYMS: deceptive, false, tricky, inaccurate
   ANTONYMS: direct, honest, true, accurate, straightforward

8. **numerous**
   ('nüm rəs)

   (adj.) many or very many
   _____Numerous_____ aunts and uncles came to our family reunion.
   SYNONYMS: several, plenty, plentiful
   ANTONYM: few

9. **productive**
   (prə 'dək tiv)

   (adj.) making or capable of making large amounts of; giving good results
   With care it may become a _____productive_____ orchard.
   SYNONYMS: energetic, effective, fruitful, efficient, worthwhile
   ANTONYMS: unproductive, idle, useless, inactive

10. **shrewd**
    (shrüd)

    (adj.) showing clever judgment and practical understanding
    My aunt is a _____shrewd_____ business woman.
    SYNONYMS: clever, artful, wise, sharp, crafty, wily, cunning
    ANTONYMS: slow, stupid, dull-witted

11. **strategy**
    ('stra tə jē)

    (n.) a carefully made plan or plot; a plan of military operations
    Our teacher suggested a test-taking _____strategy_____.
    SYNONYMS: approach, design, method, scheme

12. **villain**
    ('vi lən)

    (n.) an evil or wicked person or character, especially in a story or play
    I am going to play the _____villain_____ in the show.
    SYNONYMS: a scoundrel, rascal, outlaw, criminal
    ANTONYMS: a hero, heroine, champion

Match the Meaning

For each item choose the word whose meaning is suggested by the clue given. Then write the word in the space provided.

1. A violent or sudden attack is called a(n) _____ **assault** _____.
   a. convert   b. assault   c. strategy   d. villain

2. When I carefully make a plan, I am preparing my _____ **strategy** _____.
   a. convert   b. dispute   c. villain   d. strategy

3. People who change their religion are _____ **converts** _____ to the new religion.
   a. disputes   b. converts   c. strategies   d. villains

4. To give reasons for what you do is to _____ **justify** _____ your actions.
   a. justify   b. abandon   c. assault   d. convert

5. Some advertisements can be _____ **misleading** _____ if they leave out key details or make false claims.
   a. misleading   b. numerous   c. productive   d. impressive

6. The most wicked character in the story is the _____ **villain** _____.
   a. assault   b. dispute   c. villain   d. strategy

7. A vegetarian cookbook might give _____ **numerous** _____ recipes for rice dishes and fruit salads.
   a. productive   b. shrewd   c. misleading   d. numerous

8. To give up on something is to _____ **abandon** _____ it.
   a. assault   b. abandon   c. convert   d. justify

9. Another word for an argument or quarrel is a _____ **dispute** _____.
   a. convert   b. strategy   c. villain   d. dispute

10. A _____ **productive** _____ person is one who gets a lot done.
    a. productive   b. shrewd   c. misleading   d. impressive

11. The Grand Canyon is a(n) _____ **impressive** _____ sight.
    a. shrewd   b. misleading   c. impressive   d. numerous

12. To be clever and practical is to be _____ **shrewd** _____.
    a. misleading   b. shrewd   c. productive   d. numerous

Synonyms

*For each item below choose the word that is most nearly the **same** in meaning as the word or phrase in **boldface**. Then write your choice on the line provided.*

1. **change** starch to sugar
   a. abandon   b. assault   c. dispute   d. convert   _____ convert

2. **supported** the decision
   a. abandoned b. assaulted c. justified d. converted _____ justified

3. a **thrilling** performance
   a. misleading b. numerous c. shrewd   d. impressive _____ impressive

4. tried to be more **effective**
   a. numerous   b. misleading c. productive d. shrewd   _____ productive

5. a problem-solving **approach**
   a. strategy   b. assault   c. dispute   d. villain   _____ strategy

6. a **crafty** move
   a. misleading b. impressive c. shrewd   d. productive _____ shrewd

Antonyms

*For each item below choose the word that is most nearly **opposite** in meaning to the word or phrase in **boldface**. Then write your choice on the line provided.*

1. **agreed with** the umpire's call
   a. disputed   b. assaulted c. converted d. justified _____ disputed

2. **few** paint colors
   a. shrewd   b. misleading c. numerous d. productive _____ numerous

3. **occupy** the old shack
   a. assault   b. convert   c. abandon   d. justify   _____ abandon

4. **defended** the bridge
   a. converted b. assaulted c. disputed   d. justified _____ assaulted

5. the **hero** of the movie
   a. convert   b. assault   c. strategy   d. villain   _____ villain

6. gave **accurate** directions to the tourist
   a. impressive b. misleading c. numerous d. productive _____ misleading

Completing the Sentence

From the list of words on pages 18–19, choose the one that best completes each item below. Then write the word in the space provided. (You may have to change the word's ending.)

GREEKS AND TROJANS AT WAR

■ Both the Greek poet Homer and the Roman poet Virgil wrote of the ten-year siege of Troy by the Greeks, and of the heroes and _____**villains**_____ who did battle there.

■ One of the most famous stories describes the sly _____**strategy**_____ that the Greeks thought up to defeat the Trojans.

■ The Greeks had tried not once but on _____**numerous**_____ occasions to force the Trojans to surrender the fortress city.

■ Several times the Greeks had _____**assaulted**_____ the walls of Troy, but all of the attacks had failed.

■ Finally, the Greeks came up with a _____**shrewd**_____ plan: they left at the gates of Troy a huge wooden horse as a pretended peace offering. The Trojans brought the horse inside the city walls.

■ But the wooden horse was a _____**misleading**_____ gift, for hidden inside its huge body was a small army of Greeks, who at nightfall climbed from the horse and opened the gates to the city.

A FALSE SCIENCE

■ Alchemists were people who believed that it was possible to _____**convert**_____ ordinary metals, such as iron and lead, into gold. The best known alchemists are those who practiced in Europe during the Middle Ages.

■ They staged very _____**impressive**_____ experiments to try to convince others that they could do as they promised.

■ Some people believed that the possibility of great wealth _____**justified**_____ even the most far-fetched experiments.

■ Scientists today would _____**dispute**_____ the ideas of the alchemists, but centuries ago many people believed that their ideas were sound. In fact, it was not until the 1800s that scientists proved that base metals cannot be turned into gold.

■ Failure upon failure finally persuaded most alchemists to _____**abandon**_____ their dreams of wealth and glory.

■ In a way, the work that the alchemists did was _____**productive**_____ because it sometimes led to advances in chemistry. During the Middle Ages, for example, alchemists were responsible for the discovery of mineral acids.

Word Associations

*Circle the letter next to the word or expression that best completes the sentence or answers the question. Pay special attention to the word in **boldface**.*

1. A person who has been **abandoned**
   a. would feel powerful
   b. would feel musical
   c. would feel happy
   d. would feel lonely

2. If you **convert** a room, you
   a. leave it the same
   b. hide in it
   c. change it
   d. take a picture of it

3. You might expect a **villain** to
   a. volunteer in a soup kitchen
   b. receive an award
   c. play the cello
   d. kidnap someone

4. A really **impressive** baseball team would
   a. use extra players
   b. lack the proper equipment
   c. lead the league
   d. play only night games

5. Which might stop an **assault**?
   a. a good night's sleep
   b. a police officer
   c. a salt shaker
   d. a rocking horse

6. A winning **strategy** involves
   a. careful planning
   b. lots of money
   c. powerful friends
   d. reckless bravery

7. On a **productive** day you would
   a. play outside
   b. get a lot done
   c. stay inside
   d. get nothing done

8. If your friends are **numerous**
   a. you have very few of them
   b. they live nearby
   c. you have a lot of them
   d. they live far away

9. **Misleading** information should usually be
   a. ignored
   b. memorized
   c. published
   d. relied upon

10. When I **justify** my claims
    a. I take them back
    b. I lose them
    c. I defend them
    d. I get sued

11. A **shrewd** person would probably
    a. get lost
    b. get a good deal
    c. get a warm welcome
    d. get fooled

12. The best way to end a **dispute** is to
    a. shake hands
    b. skip lunch
    c. argue
    d. wrestle

Unit 2 ■ 23

Definitions

Study the spelling, pronunciation, part of speech, and definition given for each of the words below. Write the word in the blank space in the sentence that follows. Then read the synonyms and antonyms.

1. **bluff**
   (bləf)

   (adj.) direct and outspoken in a good-natured way
   He seemed a hearty, _____ bluff _____ *fellow.*

   (n.) a steep, high cliff or bank; an attempt to fool someone
   A scout stood on a _____ bluff _____ *overlooking the valley.*

   (v.) to deceive or trick; to try to fool others by putting on a confident front
   The thieves tried to _____ bluff _____ *their way past the security guard.*

   SYNONYMS: hearty; a ridge; a trick, hoax; to trick, mislead, pretend, fake
   ANTONYMS: insincere, artful, sly

2. **cautious**
   ('kô shəs)

   (adj.) avoiding unnecessary risks or mistakes
   A _____ cautious _____ *traveler prepares for emergencies.*

   SYNONYMS: careful, watchful, wary, guarded
   ANTONYMS: daring, reckless, wild

3. **consist**
   (kən 'sist)

   (v.) (used with *of*) to be made up of
   Many salad dressings _____ consist _____ *of oil, vinegar, and spices.*

   SYNONYMS: to contain, include, involve, comprise

4. **despise**
   (di 'spīz)

   (v.) to look down on intensely or feel contempt for, dislike strongly
   I _____ despise _____ *bullies.*

   SYNONYMS: to hate, scorn, detest, loathe
   ANTONYMS: to love, admire, esteem, adore, praise

5. **haven**
   ('hā vən)

   (n.) a safe place
   The captain sought a _____ haven _____ *from the storm.*

   SYNONYMS: a harbor, port, refuge, retreat, shelter, sanctuary
   ANTONYMS: a trap, snare, ambush

6. **miniature**
   ('mi nē ə chŭr)

   (n.) a very small copy, model, or painting
   Her collection of _____ miniatures _____ *is quite valuable.*

   (adj.) on a very small scale
   A _____ miniature _____ *railroad was on display in the toy department of the store.*

   SYNONYMS: little, tiny, minute
   ANTONYMS: huge, giant

Queen Victoria was Great Britain's **monarch** (word 7) from 1837 until 1901, when she died at the age of 81.

7. **monarch**
('mä nərk)

(n.) a person who rules over a kingdom or empire

The archbishop crowned the new _____monarch_____.

SYNONYMS: a ruler, king, queen, emperor, empress, czar, sovereign
ANTONYMS: a subject, follower, commoner

8. **obstacle**
('äb sti kəl)

(n.) something that gets in the way

Shyness need not be an _____obstacle_____ to success.

SYNONYMS: a hurdle, barrier, snag, hindrance
ANTONYMS: an aid, help, support, advantage

9. **postpone**
(pōst 'pōn)

(v.) to put off until later

Coach decided to _____postpone_____ the practice.

SYNONYMS: to delay, suspend, shelve, defer
ANTONYMS: to advance, move up

10. **straggle**
('stra gəl)

(v.) to stray off or trail behind; to spread out in a scattered fashion

Latecomers continued to _____straggle_____ into the theater.

SYNONYMS: to ramble, drift, wander, roam, rove, detour

11. **treacherous**
('tre chə rəs)

(adj.) likely to betray; seeming safe but actually dangerous

That hill can be a _____treacherous_____ climb in winter.

SYNONYMS: disloyal, untrustworthy, unreliable; chancy, deceptive, tricky, hazardous
ANTONYMS: faithful, trustworthy; safe, harmless

12. **vivid**
('vi vəd)

(adj.) bright and sharp, giving a clear picture; full of life

She gave a _____vivid_____ description of the daring rescue.

SYNONYMS: lively, intense, brilliant, dazzling, sharp, spirited, clear
ANTONYMS: lifeless, dull, drab, hazy, foggy

Match the Meaning

For each item below, choose the word whose meaning is suggested by the clue given. Then write the word in the space provided.

1. A picture so brilliant and bold that it seems alive might be called _____vivid_____.
   a. bluff   b. cautious   c. treacherous   d. vivid

2. A sundae _____consists_____ of ice cream and your choice of toppings.
   a. despises   b. consists   c. postpones   d. straggles

3. Something that blocks our way might be called a(n) _____obstacle_____.
   a. obstacle   b. bluff   c. haven   d. miniature

4. Hikers who stray from a trail or fall behind are guilty of _____straggling_____.
   a. consisting   b. despising   c. straggling   d. postponing

5. To try to fool others by acting very confident is to _____bluff_____.
   a. consist   b. despise   c. straggle   d. bluff

6. If you _____postpone_____ doing a chore, you will just have to do it later.
   a. bluff   b. postpone   c. straggle   d. despise

7. Walking on a decaying log that bridges a stream could be _____treacherous_____.
   a. treacherous   b. cautious   c. miniature   d. bluff

8. To hate or to dislike something strongly is to _____despise_____ it.
   a. postpone   b. bluff   c. despise   d. consist

9. Another name for king is _____monarch_____.
   a. haven   b. bluff   c. monarch   d. miniature

10. Boats seek a safe _____haven_____ where they can drop anchor for the night.
    a. bluff   b. obstacle   c. monarch   d. haven

11. A tiny copy of a full-sized object is known as a _____miniature_____.
    a. bluff   b. miniature   c. haven   d. monarch

12. To avoid unnecessary risk is to act in a _____cautious_____ way.
    a. cautious   b. vivid   c. miniature   d. treacherous

26 ■ Unit 3

Synonyms

*For each item below choose the word that is most nearly the same in meaning as the word or phrase in **boldface**. Then write your choice on the line provided.*

1. **fake** your way past the guard
   a. consist   b. despise   c. postpone   d. bluff   _____ bluff _____

2. **wander** from the route
   a. bluff   b. straggle   c. postpone   d. despise   _____ straggle _____

3. a peaceful **refuge** in the war-torn city
   a. haven   b. miniature   c. monarch   d. bluff   _____ haven _____

4. said our best chance **involved** surprise
   a. bluffed   b. consisted of   c. despised   d. postponed   _____ consisted of _____

5. a **watchful** driver
   a. miniature   b. treacherous   c. cautious   d. vivid   _____ cautious _____

6. a noble, wise, and generous **ruler**
   a. monarch   b. haven   c. obstacle   d. miniature   _____ monarch _____

Antonyms

*For each item below choose the word that is most nearly opposite in meaning to the word or phrase in **boldface**. Then write your choice on the line provided.*

1. **adore** that kind of music
   a. consist   b. bluff   c. despise   d. straggle   _____ despise _____

2. formed a **hazy** image
   a. treacherous   b. vivid   c. cautious   d. miniature   _____ vivid _____

3. to **move up** the ceremony one month
   a. postpone   b. bluff   c. despise   d. straggle   _____ postpone _____

4. a **huge** model of the castle
   a. cautious   b. treacherous   c. bluff   d. miniature   _____ miniature _____

5. a **faithful** servant
   a. treacherous   b. cautious   c. miniature   d. vivid   _____ treacherous _____

6. no **advantage** to winning the election
   a. haven   b. obstacle   c. miniature   d. monarch   _____ obstacle _____

Completing the Sentence

From the list of words on pages 24–25, choose the one that best completes each item below. Then write the word in the space provided. (You may have to change the word's ending.)

AMERICANS FIGHT FOR THEIR INDEPENDENCE

■ King George III was the English _____**monarch**_____ when American colonists began to grow impatient with English rule.

■ Even colonists who were eager for independence were _____**cautious**_____ at first because they did not want a war.

■ But not all colonists _____**despised**_____ British rule; nearly one-third of them believed they should stay loyal to the King.

■ The first fight took place between 700 British soldiers and a small army that _____**consisted**_____ of 70 American volunteers called Minutemen. The site of the battle was Lexington, Massachusetts.

■ In 1780, the American General Benedict Arnold took part in a _____**treacherous**_____ plot that nearly cost the lives of three thousand American soldiers.

■ After overcoming many _____**obstacles**_____, the Americans defeated the British, and King George recognized the United States as an independent nation.

A VIEW FROM HIGH ABOVE

■ As we looked down from the rocky _____**bluff**_____, we could see a small herd of wild ponies trotting in a field far below us.

■ We were so high above them that they looked like _____**miniature**_____ horses.

■ One gray mare _____**straggled**_____ behind the rest of the herd to protect her young foal.

A GETAWAY FOR PRESIDENTS

■ Since 1942, American presidents have used a quiet cabin retreat in Maryland as a _____**haven**_____ from the summer heat of Washington, D.C.

■ My Uncle David has _____**vivid**_____ memories of the occasion when President Eisenhower renamed the retreat Camp David to honor the President's grandson.

■ A crisis might cause the President to _____**postpone**_____ a planned visit to Camp David until the situation is under control.

Word Associations

*Circle the letter next to the word or expression that best completes the sentence or answers the question. Pay special attention to the word in **boldface**.*

1. A **vivid** performance by an actor
   a. would bore you
   b. would anger you
   c. would entertain you
   d. would disappoint you

2. A **treacherous** classmate might
   a. reveal your secrets
   b. be good at science
   c. eat too much at lunch
   d. forget to wear a bike helmet

3. A person who overcomes **obstacles**
   a. is a fast runner
   b. enjoys swimming
   c. rarely follows through
   d. does not give up easily

4. If you **straggle** on a field trip
   a. you go home early
   b. you lead the way
   c. you learn a lot
   d. you might get lost

5. A cool **haven** on a hot afternoon might be
   a. a steam bath
   b. a desert
   c. a shady tree
   d. a wool sweater

6. Some people **bluff** when they
   a. take a stroll along a cliff
   b. have lunch
   c. watch television
   d. play a game

7. If you **despise** something
   a. you are surprised by it
   b. you absolutely hate it
   c. you don't care about it
   d. you like it very much

8. A **miniature** dog would probably
   a. be a good hunter
   b. eat you out of house and home
   c. have a nasty temper
   d. be small enough to hold

9. Of what does a pizza **consist**?
   a. crust, sauce, and cheese
   b. a good appetite
   c. Italian restaurants
   d. about a dollar a slice

10. Which might be **postponed** because of rain?
    a. a hockey game
    b. a football game
    c. a baseball game
    d. a basketball game

11. A **cautious** skier would probably
    a. ski only at night
    b. stay on the beginner's slopes
    c. buy used equipment
    d. perform dangerous stunts

12. Which would a **monarch** wear?
    a. a parka
    b. a baseball hat
    c. a crown
    d. a bathing suit

Definitions

Study the spelling, pronunciation, part of speech, and definition given for each of the words below. Write the word in the blank space in the sentence that follows. Then read the synonyms and antonyms.

1. **aggressive**
   (ə 'gre siv)

   (adj.) quick to fight or quarrel, tending to violence; bold and forceful, determined

   An _____**aggressive**_____ salesperson never gives up.

   SYNONYMS: violent, warlike; bold, pushy, forceful, vigorous
   ANTONYMS: peaceful, timid; shy, bashful, retiring

2. **associate**
   (v., ə 'sō shē āt;
   n., adj., ə 'sō shē
   ət)

   (v.) to join or be together as partners, allies, or friends; to link in one's mind, connect

   I will always _____**associate**_____ peaches with summer.

   (n.) a partner, friend

   The businessman introduced his _____**associate**_____.

   (adj.) having less than full rank

   She was hired as an _____**associate**_____ professor in the English department.

   SYNONYMS: to unite, mingle, combine, mix, relate; a companion, teammate, co-worker; an assistant
   ANTONYMS: to separate, distance, divorce; an enemy, foe, rival, stranger

3. **deceive**
   (di 'sēv)

   (v.) to trick or lead a person into believing something that is not true

   It is unfair to _____**deceive**_____ the customer with false advertising.

   SYNONYMS: to fool, swindle, mislead, double-cross, cheat

4. **emigrate**
   ('e mə grāt)

   (v.) to leave one's home country or area to live in another

   Henri hopes to _____**emigrate**_____ from Haiti to the United States.

   SYNONYMS: to relocate, resettle, move, migrate

5. **flexible**
   ('flek sə bəl)

   (adj.) able to bend without breaking; able to change or to take in new ideas

   I brought in a box of _____**flexible**_____ straws.

   SYNONYMS: bendable, limber, elastic, springy; adaptable, adjustable
   ANTONYMS: stiff, rigid, unbendable; inflexible

6. **glamour**
   ('gla mər)

   (n.) mysterious charm, beauty or attractiveness

   The movie captures the _____**glamour**_____ of Paris.

   SYNONYMS: style, sparkle, magic, enchantment, romance, fascination

The main **span** (word 12) of the Golden Gate Bridge is 4,200 feet in length. When it was completed in 1937, it was the longest suspension bridge in the world.

7. **hazy**
('hā zē)

(adj.) unclear, misty; not readily seen or understandable
Another hot and _____ hazy _____ day is forecast.
SYNONYMS: cloudy, smoggy, foggy, blurry, dim; vague
ANTONYMS: bright, clear; precise

8. **linger**
('liŋ gər)

(v.) to stay longer than expected, be slow in leaving; to go slowly or take one's time
We like to _____ linger _____ over breakfast on Saturdays.
SYNONYMS: to delay, stall, remain, stay, lag, persist; to dawdle
ANTONYMS: to hurry, rush, charge, hasten

9. **luxurious**
(ləg 'zhŭr ē əs)

(adj.) providing ease and comfort far beyond what is ordinary or necessary
They took a _____ luxurious _____ vacation.
SYNONYMS: rich, elegant, pleasurable, lavish, extravagant, fancy
ANTONYMS: poor, plain, simple, modest

10. **mishap**
('mis hap)

(n.) an unfortunate but minor accident
The waiters chuckled over the _____ mishap _____.
SYNONYMS: a misfortune, mistake, blunder, slipup

11. **overwhelm**
(ō vər 'welm)

(v.) to overcome by superior force, crush; to affect so deeply as to make helpless
Fresh troops threatened to _____ overwhelm _____ the weakened defenders.
SYNONYMS: to overpower, destroy, crush; to stun, shock, stagger, astound

12. **span**
(span)

(n.) the full reach or length, especially between two points in space or time
The _____ span _____ of most insects' lives is very brief.
(v.) to stretch or reach across
A new bridge will be built to _____ span _____ the river.
SYNONYMS: extent, distance, length, scope, period; to bridge, connect, cross, last

Match the Meaning

For each item choose the word whose meaning is suggested by the clue given. Then write the word in the space provided.

1. People who are too _____ **aggressive** _____ often get into quarrels or fights.
   a. flexible   b. hazy   c. luxurious   d. aggressive

2. To fool people into believing what is not true is to _____ **deceive** _____ them.
   a. overwhelm   b. deceive   c. emigrate   d. linger

3. If you join with me as a partner, you _____ **associate** _____ with me.
   a. associate   b. deceive   c. overwhelm   d. span

4. It is not easy to see distant mountains on a(n) _____ **hazy** _____ day.
   a. aggressive   b. flexible   c. hazy   d. luxurious

5. A princess's charm and beauty might make her a symbol of _____ **glamour** _____.
   a. associate   b. mishap   c. span   d. glamour

6. To _____ **emigrate** _____ from Korea to Nepal is to leave Korea to live in Nepal.
   a. associate   b. emigrate   c. linger   d. overwhelm

7. Getting a paper cut is an example of a minor _____ **mishap** _____.
   a. mishap   b. span   c. associate   d. glamour

8. A mighty army might easily _____ **overwhelm** _____ a weaker foe.
   a. emigrate   b. linger   c. overwhelm   d. associate

9. A _____ **flexible** _____ straw makes it easy to drink from a juice box.
   a. luxurious   b. aggressive   c. flexible   d. hazy

10. A _____ **luxurious** _____ hotel might provide six fluffy bath towels for each guest.
    a. aggressive   b. hazy   c. flexible   d. luxurious

11. To stay longer than expected or to leave slowly is to _____ **linger** _____.
    a. deceive   b. linger   c. emigrate   d. span

12. A bridge that crosses the Mississippi is said to _____ **span** _____ that river.
    a. span   b. associate   c. linger   d. overwhelm

Synonyms

*For each item below choose the word that is most nearly the **same** in meaning as the word or phrase in **boldface**. Then write your choice on the line provided.*

1. the **magic** of Hollywood
   a. mishap   b. span   c. glamour   d. associate   _____ glamour _____

2. **crush** our opponents
   a. deceive   b. emigrate   c. linger   d. overwhelm   _____ overwhelm _____

3. told us about the **slipup**
   a. glamour   b. span   c. mishap   d. associate   _____ mishap _____

4. **move** from Egypt to Italy
   a. overwhelm   b. linger   c. deceive   d. emigrate   _____ emigrate _____

5. **mislead** the enemy
   a. associate   b. deceive   c. overwhelm   d. emigrate   _____ deceive _____

6. over the **period** of a year
   a. associate   b. mishap   c. span   d. glamour   _____ span _____

Antonyms

*For each item below choose the word that is most nearly **opposite** in meaning to the word or phrase in **boldface**. Then write your choice on the line provided.*

1. **timid** base runners
   a. associate   b. aggressive   c. luxurious   d. hazy   _____ aggressive _____

2. introduced her **rival**
   a. glamour   b. associate   c. span   d. mishap   _____ associate _____

3. **hurry** over our good-byes
   a. span   b. emigrate   c. overwhelm   d. linger   _____ linger _____

4. a **rigid** point of view
   a. flexible   b. aggressive   c. hazy   d. luxurious   _____ flexible _____

5. a **simple** meal with friends
   a. aggressive   b. flexible   c. luxurious   d. hazy   _____ luxurious _____

6. a **clear** sky
   a. flexible   b. luxurious   c. aggressive   d. hazy   _____ hazy _____

Completing the Sentence

From the list of words on pages 30–31, choose the one that best completes each item below. Then write the word in the space provided. (You may have to change the word's ending.)

A NEW LIFE IN AMERICA

■ Poor conditions in their homeland have driven many Mexicans to _____**emigrate**_____ to the United States. Many have settled in the Southwest, but others have traveled to big cities in the Midwest and Northeast in search of work.

■ Some dishonest agents _____**deceive**_____ travelers by taking their money in exchange for legal documents that they never provide.

■ Over the _____**span**_____ of the past fifty years, more immigrants have come to the U.S. from Mexico than from any other country.

■ Many immigrants have only a(n) _____**hazy**_____ notion of what life will be like in the new country they have heard so much about.

■ Mix-ups over language or local customs often lead to _____**mishaps**_____ and misunderstandings.

■ Despite facing some _____**overwhelming**_____ problems, most immigrants manage to build better lives for themselves and their families.

A LEGAL BRIEF

■ It is a lawyer's duty to act in a(n) _____**aggressive**_____ fashion in order to protect the interests of his or her clients. Trial lawyers especially cannot afford to be timid or shy.

■ Most lawyers, like other professionals, have to keep _____**flexible**_____ hours in order to serve their clients well.

■ From the newest _____**associate**_____ to senior partners, lawyers must research past cases to find ways to support their arguments. For this reason they often spend long hours in law libraries.

■ Media attention lends some legal cases more _____**glamour**_____ than they really deserve. Some especially newsworthy trials are now televised from start to finish.

■ The impact of such cases may _____**linger**_____ in the public mind long after all the lawyers, the judge, and the jurors have left the courtroom.

■ Lawyers on television and in movies are often seen to drive _____**luxurious**_____ cars and wear expensive clothes. In fact, most real-life lawyers work long, hard hours and rarely enjoy the spotlight of celebrity.

*Circle the letter next to the word or expression that best completes the sentence or answers the question. Pay special attention to the word in **boldface**.*

1. Which is an example of a **mishap**?
   a. solving a riddle
   b. a serious car accident
   c. stepping in a puddle
   d. telling a lie

2. If a movie **overwhelms** you, you
   a. might feel like you will cry
   b. might ask for a refund
   c. might refuse to clap
   d. might get very hungry

3. If you have a **hazy** grasp of map reading, you should
   a. use a brighter lamp
   b. memorize the state capitals
   c. take the bus
   d. learn more about keys and symbols

4. You might **linger** if you are
   a. not wearing a watch
   b. late for an appointment
   c. having a great time
   d. bored to tears

5. A **luxurious** outfit might include
   a. gold jewelry
   b. rags
   c. T-shirts
   d. aluminum foil

6. Which would most people **associate**?
   a. bicycles with snowshoes
   b. winter with fireworks
   c. fishing with homework
   d. vacations with summer

7. In a place known for **glamour,** a visitor might find
   a. cows grazing in a field
   b. unpaved roads
   c. lots of factories
   d. expensive restaurants

8. **aggressive** ball players would
   a. lose interest in the game
   b. play as hard as they can
   c. let their opponents win
   d. ask to sit out the game

9. You might **deceive** a puppy by
   a. pretending to throw a ball
   b. taking off its collar
   c. feeding it twice a day
   d. changing your clothes

10. A U.S. citizen might **emigrate** to
    a. the moon
    b. Florida
    c. Canada
    d. New York City

11. The "**span** of a lifetime" means
    a. from Monday to Friday
    b. from birth to death
    c. from kindergarten to college
    d. from breakfast to dinner

12. Which is the most **flexible**?
    a. a frying pan
    b. a pipe wrench
    c. an extension ladder
    d. a garden hose

Selecting Word Meanings

*For each of the following items circle the choice that is most nearly the **same** in meaning as the word in **boldface**.*

1. a **myth** about the beginning of Rome
   a. fact   (b.) legend   c. trial   d. doubt

2. a **flexible** kind of plastic
   a. rigid   b. fireproof   (c.) elastic   d. slippery

3. **deceived** his partner
   a. honored   b. amused   c. soothed   (d.) double-crossed

4. a witness to the **assault**
   (a.) attack   b. accident   c. joke   d. agreement

5. **overwhelm** the enemy
   a. entertain   (b.) crush   c. outrun   d. trick

6. **reject** the application
   a. study   b. accept   c. forget   (d.) decline

7. climbed the **bluff**
   a. stairs   b. tower   (c.) bank   d. ladder

8. a **haven** for travelers
   a. map   b. show   (c.) refuge   d. tour

9. **linger** near home
   (a.) remain   b. play   c. hide   d. dig

10. **despise** cruelty to animals
    a. admire   b. outlaw   (c.) detest   d. fear

11. **abandon** the house
    a. build   b. occupy   (c.) desert   d. watch

12. a **vivid** picture
    a. small and   b. dark and   (c.) bright and   d. famous and
       blurry   gloomy   colorful   expensive

For each item below study the **boldface** word in which there is a blank.
If a letter is missing, fill in the blank to make a correctly spelled word.
If the word is already spelled correctly, leave the blank empty.

1. **em _i_ grate** from India

2. a **min _i_ ature** poodle

3. **stra _g_ gle** into class

4. a sudden **mis _h_ ap**

5. a government **do _c_ ument**

6. a confusing **strate __ gy**

7. **con _s_ ist** of bread and water

8. a **solit _a_ ry** ladybug

9. an **impres _s_ ive** score

10. **span __** the stream

11. a **tempor _a_ ry** arrangement

12. the sneaky **vi _l_ lain**

Antonyms

For each of the following items circle the choice that is most nearly
the **opposite** in meaning to the word in **boldface**.

1. a **continuous** line
   a. short   b. thin   (c.) broken   d. thick

2. **justify** my decision to move
   a. defend   b. explain   (c.) question   d. regret

3. **veteran** tournament players
   (a.) inexperienced   b. skilled   c. popular   d. seasoned

4. **numerous** students
   a. many   b. happy   c. angry   (d.) few

5. a **productive** day
   a. cool   b. fruitful   (c.) inactive   d. memorable

6. turned out to be an **obstacle**
   (a.) advantage   b. enemy   c. problem   d. echo

7. **postpone** a decision
   a. delay   (b.) hasten   c. question   d. change

8. a **hazy** memory of the accident
   a. sad   b. dim   c. disturbing   (d.) clear

Words have been left out of the following passage. For each numbered item in the passage, fill in the circle next to the word in the margin that best fills the blank space. Then answer each question below by writing a sentence that contains one of the words you have chosen.

Virginia, England's first colony in North America, was founded in 1607 at Jamestown. The ocean voyage from England to North America was long and dangerous, so the leaders of the colony lured Englishmen to Virginia with __1__ promises of wealth.

Many of the first settlers were disappointed when they arrived. They did not become wealthy and they faced many hardships. The land was swampy and home to mosquitoes. The colonists led a very __2__ existence; harsh weather and food shortages put the colony's future in doubt. Many suffered from disease, hunger, and cold. During the first year, half of the original settlers died.

In order to attract new settlers, the leaders of Virginia promised to __3__ fifty acres of land to anyone who would come to the colony to live. Hoping to get land, thousands of the English sailed to Virginia between 1618 and 1622. By 1619, Virginia had its own assembly. Tobacco became an important industry. As the colony grew, the settlers and Native Americans got into __4__ over land.

In 1622, war broke out between the Native Americans and settlers. By 1625, the fighting was over. The settlers had won, and the Virginia colony had survived.

1. ○ temporary
   ● misleading
   ○ cautious
   ○ flexible

2. ● fragile
   ○ luxurious
   ○ impressive
   ○ productive

3. ○ despise
   ○ postpone
   ○ cancel
   ● distribute

4. ● disputes
   ○ documents
   ○ blunders
   ○ havens

5. What happened between settlers and Native Americans as the Virginia colony grew?

   The settlers and Native Americans got into **disputes** over land.

6. What did the leaders of Virginia do to attract new settlers to the colony after 1618?

   The leaders promised to **distribute** fifty acres of land to anybody who came to the colony to live.

7. How did harsh weather and food shortages affect the colonists in Virginia?

   The colonists led a very **fragile** existence.

8. How did the leaders of the colony persuade the first settlers to come to Virginia?

   The leaders made **misleading** promises to the settlers.

Analogies

In each of the following circle the letter for the item that best completes the comparison. Then explain the relationship on the lines provided. The first one has been done for you.

1. **cautious** is to **careful** as
   a. numerous is to simple
   b. continuous is to ugly
   c. aggressive is to forceful
   d. misleading is to true

   Relationship: <u>"Cautious" and "careful" are</u> <u>synonyms (or have the same meaning);</u> <u>"aggressive" and "forceful" are</u> <u>synonyms (or have the same meaning).</u>

2. **shrewd** is to **foolish** as
   a. high is to towering
   b. happy is to sad
   c. spotless is to neat
   d. famous is to rich

   Relationship: <u>"Shrewd" and "foolish" are</u> <u>opposites/antonyms; "happy" and "sad"</u> <u>are opposites/antonyms.</u>

3. **mistake** is to **blunder** as
   a. obstacle is to opening
   b. glamour is to wealth
   c. myth is to history
   d. outlaw is to villain

   Relationship: <u>"Mistake" and "blunder" are</u> <u>synonyms/have the same meaning;</u> <u>"outlaw" and "villain" are synonyms/</u> <u>have the same meaning.</u>

4. **monarch** is to **kingdom** as
   a. veteran is to war
   b. villain is to hero
   c. mayor is to city
   d. senator is to election

   Relationship: <u>A monarch governs a</u> <u>kingdom; a mayor governs a city.</u>

Challenge: Make up your own

Write a comparison using the words in the box below. (Hint: There are four possible analogies.) Then write the relationship on the lines provided. One comparison has been completed for you.

fragile	lion	calf	lamb
flexible	rabbit	break	burrow
sheep	den	cow	bend

Analogy: <u>lion</u> is to <u>den</u> as <u>rabbit</u> is to <u>burrow</u>.
Relationship: <u>A lion lives in a den; a rabbit lives in a burrow.</u>

Analogy: _____ is to _____ as _____ is to _____.
Relationship: <u>See Table of Contents</u>

Word Families

*The words in **boldface** in the sentences below are related to words introduced in Units 1–4. For example, the nouns justification and cancellation in item 1 are related to the verbs justify (Unit 2) and cancel (Unit 1). Based on your understanding of the unit words that follow, circle the related word in **boldface** that best completes each sentence.*

distribute	glamour	postpone	emigrate	cancel
aggressive	deceive	justify	myth	cautious
straggle	flexible	document	associate	reject
convert	strategy	treacherous	consist	luxurious

1. Blizzard conditions led to the (**justification**/**cancellation**) of flights throughout the upper Midwest.

2. Unicorns and dragons are classic examples of (**mythical**/**strategic**) animals.

3. The potato famine of the 1840s led to the (**flexibility**/**emigration**) of hundreds of thousands of Irish to the United States.

4. One should always use extreme (**caution**/**distribution**) when approaching a wild animal.

5. Our guide warned the (**associations**/**stragglers**) that they might get lost if they didn't keep up with the rest of the tour group.

6. The traitor Benedict Arnold is better known for his (**treachery**/**luxury**) than for his earlier service to the American cause.

7. A buyer of a painting by an Old Master will want to see some (**aggression**/**documentation**) that proves it is not a fake.

8. The melted ice cream tasted sweet but had the (**consistency**/**postponement**) of soup.

9. The downtown areas of some cities are coming to life once again thanks to the (**conversion**/**rejection**) of old factory buildings into shops and housing.

10. Some who go to Hollywood in search of fame and fortune find that life there is not so (**deceptive**/**glamorous**) as they have been led to believe.

Word Games

Use the clue and the given letters to complete each word. Write the missing letters of the word in the appropriate boxes. Then use the circled letters and the drawing to answer the CHALLENGE question below.

1. Not to be trusted

T R E (A) C H E R O U S

2. Tending to use force or violence

A G G R E S S I (V) E

3. Constant or unbroken

C O N T (I) N U O U S

4. A brief tussle or fist fight

S C U F F (L) E

5. A king or queen

M O (N) A R C H

6. Rich and elegant

(L) U X U R I O U S

7. Mix or join with

A S S O C (I) A T E

Challenge:

What am I?

V I L L A I N

Definitions

Study the spelling, pronunciation, part of speech, and definition given for each of the words below. Write the word in the blank space in the sentence that follows. Then read the synonyms and antonyms.

1. **blemish**
('ble mish)

(n.) a mark or stain that damages the appearance of something; a weakness or flaw

The carpenter noticed a _____ blemish _____ in the finish of the cabinet.

SYNONYMS: a scar, spot, smudge; a defect, weak spot

2. **blunt**
(blənt)

(adj.) having a dull point or edge, not sharp; honest but insensitive in manner

My uncle gave me some _____ blunt _____ advice.

(v.) to make less sharp

Misuse will _____ blunt _____ a knife blade.

SYNONYMS: dull; outspoken, frank, direct
ANTONYMS: sharp, keen; tactful, diplomatic; to sharpen

3. **capable**
('kā pə bəl)

(adj.) able and prepared to do something; fit or skilled

A _____ capable _____ teacher should be rewarded.

SYNONYMS: qualified, able
ANTONYMS: unqualified, incapable, unfit

4. **conclude**
(kən 'klüd)

(v.) to finish; to bring something to an end; to decide after careful thought

After electing a new secretary, the committee voted to _____ conclude _____ the meeting.

SYNONYMS: to close, complete, stop; to reason, judge
ANTONYMS: to open, begin, start, commence

5. **detect**
(di 'tekt)

(v.) to find or discover something, notice

A test may _____ detect _____ chemicals in the water supply.

SYNONYMS: to find, observe, spot
ANTONYMS: to miss, overlook

6. **fatigue**
(fə 'tēg)

(n.) weariness or exhaustion from work or lack of sleep

By the end of the day I felt overcome with _____ fatigue _____.

(v.) to make very tired

The riders were warned not to _____ fatigue _____ the horses.

SYNONYMS: tiredness, sleepiness, weakness; to tire
ANTONYMS: liveliness, energy; to energize, perk up

A Bedouin is shown here leading camels across the desert. Bedouins are **nomads** (word 9) who speak Arabic and live in the Middle East.

7. **festive**
   ('fes tiv)

(adj.) having to do with a feast or celebration
   Decorations will help lend a _____ festive _____ *atmosphere.*
   SYNONYMS: happy, merry, playful
   ANTONYMS: sad, gloomy, somber

8. **hospitality**
   (häs pə 'ta lə tē)

(n.) a friendly welcome and treatment of guests
   The innkeepers were famous for their _____ hospitality _____.
   SYNONYMS: friendliness, generosity, warmth
   ANTONYMS: unfriendliness, hostility

9. **nomad**
   ('nō mad)

(n.) a member of a people who move from place to place; a person who roams aimlessly
   The adventurer lived the life of a _____ nomad _____.
   SYNONYMS: a wanderer, roamer, rover

10. **persecute**
    ('pər si kyüt)

(v.) to treat unjustly or cause to suffer
   Dictators often try to _____ persecute _____ *minority.*
   SYNONYMS: to torment, hurt, annoy, pester
   ANTONYMS: to reward, favor, comfort, help, protect

11. **supreme**
    (sə 'prēm)

(adj.) highest in power, rank, authority, quality, or degree
   He acted as if giving up his seat were the _____ supreme _____ *sacrifice.*
   SYNONYMS: first, greatest, dominant, outstanding
   ANTONYMS: low, lowly, worst

12. **transport**
    (*v.,* trans 'pōrt;
    n., 'trans pōrt)

(v.) to move or carry from one place to another
   A mover was hired to _____ transport _____ *the furniture.*
   (n.) a vehicle used to move things from place to place; the act or process of moving something from one place to another
   The ocean liner was used as troop _____ transport _____ *during the war.*
   SYNONYMS: to carry, haul, cart, send, convey

Match the Meaning

For each item choose the word whose meaning is suggested by the clue given. Then write the word in the space provided.

1. People who never settle down in one place are called _____ **nomads** _____.
   a. blemishes   b. fatigues   c. hospitalities   d. nomads

2. To _____ **persecute** _____ someone is to be cruel to that person.
   a. conclude   b. persecute   c. blunt   d. detect

3. To prove your ability at something is to show yourself _____ **capable** _____.
   a. capable   b. festive   c. supreme   d. blunt

4. A train is a good form of _____ **transport** _____ if you want to enjoy the scenery.
   a. nomad   b. transport   c. blemish   d. fatigue

5. Weddings and birthdays are examples of _____ **festive** _____ events.
   a. blunt   b. capable   c. festive   d. supreme

6. To notice something is to _____ **detect** _____ it.
   a. detect   b. conclude   c. persecute   d. blunt

7. You can usually overcome _____ **fatigue** _____ by getting a good night's sleep.
   a. transport   b. hospitality   c. fatigue   d. blemishes

8. The _____ **Supreme** _____ Court is the highest in the land.
   a. Supreme   b. Blunt   c. Festive   d. Capable

9. It's a good idea to _____ **conclude** _____ a speech with a summary.
   a. blunt   b. conclude   c. detect   d. persecute

10. A smudge in a paint job is an example of a _____ **blemish** _____.
    a. hospitality   b. transport   c. nomad   d. blemish

11. Improper use of a knife may _____ **blunt** _____ its edge.
    a. detect   b. transport   c. blunt   d. conclude

12. Good hosts would be sure to show _____ **hospitality** _____.
    a. transport   b. hospitality   c. blemish   d. fatigue

Synonyms

*For each item below choose the word that is most nearly the **same** in meaning as the word or phrase in **boldface**. Then write your choice on the line provided.*

1. her **outstanding** accomplishment
   a. blunt   b. festive   c. supreme   d. capable   _____supreme_____

2. tried to conceal the **flaw**
   a. blemish   b. nomad   c. fatigue   d. hospitality   _____blemish_____

3. **carry** the grain to distant markets
   a. conclude   b. detect   c. blunt   d. transport   _____transport_____

4. a **skilled** performer, but not a star
   a. supreme   b. capable   c. blunt   d. festive   _____capable_____

5. followed the trail of **wanderers**
   a. transports   b. fatigue   c. nomads   d. hospitalities   _____nomads_____

6. a **happy** atmosphere
   a. festive   b. capable   c. supreme   d. blunt   _____festive_____

Antonyms

*For each item below choose the word that is most nearly **opposite** in meaning to the word or phrase in **boldface**. Then write your choice on the line provided.*

1. **overlook** the danger
   a. detect   b. conclude   c. persecute   d. transport   _____detect_____

2. spoke in a **diplomatic** manner
   a. supreme   b. festive   c. blunt   d. capable   _____blunt_____

3. **begin** the homework project
   a. detect   b. persecute   c. transport   d. conclude   _____conclude_____

4. **protected** the strangers
   a. blunted   b. persecuted   c. concluded   d. detected   _____persecuted_____

5. surprised by their **liveliness**
   a. nomad   b. blemish   c. fatigue   d. hospitality   _____fatigue_____

6. showed **unfriendliness** to the visitors
   a. fatigue   b. hospitality   c. transports   d. blemishes   _____hospitality_____

 **Completing the Sentence**

From the list of words on pages 42–43, choose the one that best completes each item below. Then write the word in the space provided. (You may have to change the word's ending.)

SPEAKING OUT AGAINST BIAS

■ The principal did not mince her words but spoke in _____**blunt**_____ terms on the subject of prejudice to the students assembled in the school auditorium.

■ She described the ugly insult that had been written on a wall as a _____**blemish**_____ on the school's honor.

■ She went on to warn that she would not allow a handful of students to be _____**persecuted**_____ just because they held different religious beliefs from most.

■ "Sometimes it requires a _____**supreme**_____ effort," she said, "to overcome our prejudices and respect the diginity of others. But it is an effort that all civilized people must make."

■ She asked that everyone work together to make ours a school that is known for the _____**hospitality**_____ it shows to all.

ON THE MOVE

■ Though many Native American peoples lived in settled villages and tilled the land, many others lived the life of _____**nomads**_____.

■ The nomadic tribes of the Great Plains marked successful buffalo hunts with _____**festive**_____ ceremonies of thanks.

■ In Asia the nomadic Kazakhs use camels to _____**transport**_____ their tents, called yurts, and other belongings from place to place.

■ Because they lose body water very slowly, camels are _____**capable**_____ of traveling for days, even in extreme heat, without drinking a drop. When they do have water to drink, they can consume as much as 25 gallons in ten minutes!

A TRAIN DERAILS

■ The safety panel looking into the train crash _____**concluded**_____ that the most likely cause was human error.

■ It was learned that the engineer had not slept in over 36 hours and was probably suffering from extreme _____**fatigue**_____.

■ Furthermore, tests of the equipment did not _____**detect**_____ any signs of failure in the train's braking system.

 **Word Associations**

*Circle the letter next to the word or expression that best completes the sentence or answers the question. Pay special attention to the word in **boldface**.*

1. If you feel **fatigue**, you might
   a. take a nap
   b. run 3 miles
   c. swim 50 laps
   d. clean out the garage

2. Which *cannot* offer **hospitality**?
   a. a school
   b. a gift box
   c. a town
   d. a person

3. Someone who is **blunt** might
   a. cheer you up
   b. hurt your feelings
   c. lie to you
   d. forget your birthday

4. Which is a **festive** event?
   a. a final exam
   b. a terrible tragedy
   c. a birthday party
   d. a criminal trial

5. A **capable** student is one who
   a. travels a long way to school
   b. misses a lot of school
   c. does well in school
   d. knows everyone in school

6. Which of the following might you use to **detect** something?
   a. a pencil
   b. a magnifying glass
   c. a sandwich
   d. a pair of scissors

7. A **blemished** jewel will probably
   a. cost less than a flawless one
   b. be stolen
   c. be found in a museum
   d. cost more than a flawless one

8. A good detective might **conclude** a robbery case by
   a. turning in her badge
   b. looking for clues
   c. having donuts and coffee
   d. arresting the thief

9. Your **supreme** achievement is
   a. your greatest
   b. your worst
   c. your first
   d. your last

10. A **nomad's** home might be
    a. an apartment
    b. a castle
    c. a tent
    d. a farmhouse

11. If I were **persecuted,** I would
    a. feel happy
    b. feel hungry
    c. feel hurt
    d. feel sleepy

12. Which might **transport** an elephant?
    a. a skateboard
    b. a shopping cart
    c. a hot-air balloon
    d. a big truck

Definitions *Study the spelling, pronunciation, part of speech, and definition given for each of the words below. Write the word in the blank space in the sentence that follows. Then read the synonyms and antonyms.*

1. **accomplish**
   (ə 'käm plish)

   (v.) to do, make happen, succeed in, carry through
   Let's work together to _____accomplish_____ the task.

   SYNONYMS: to perform, fulfill, achieve, complete
   ANTONYMS: to fail, undo, fall short

2. **apparent**
   (ə 'par ənt)

   (adj.) open to view; easy to understand; seeming to be true or real
   Speeding was the _____apparent_____ cause of the accident.

   SYNONYMS: clear, obvious, visible; plain; likely, seeming
   ANTONYMS: hidden, concealed; difficult, uncertain

3. **capacity**
   (kə 'pa sə tē)

   (n.) the amount of space that can be filled; ability or skill; office or role
   The stadium was filled to _____capacity_____ for the championship game.

   SYNONYMS: volume, size, room; gift, ability; position, job

4. **civilian**
   (sə 'vil yən)

   (n.) a person not on active duty in a military, police, or firefighting force
   A team of _____civilians_____ investigated the accident.
   (adj.) non-military
   No _____civilian_____ casualties were reported.

   SYNONYM: non-military
   ANTONYM: military

5. **conceal**
   (kən 'sēl)

   (v.) to hide or keep secret, to place out of sight
   I tried to _____conceal_____ my disappointment with a smile.

   SYNONYMS: to cover, disguise, mask, tuck away
   ANTONYMS: to uncover, open, reveal

6. **duplicate**
   (*v.*, 'dü pli kāt;
   n., adj., 'dü pli kət)

   (v.) to copy exactly; to produce something equal to
   A locksmith can _____duplicate_____ almost any key.
   (adj.) exactly like something else
   My friend and I came up with _____duplicate_____ answers.
   (n.) an exact copy
   He hung up a framed _____duplicate_____ of a famous painting in his office.

   SYNONYMS: to reproduce, clone; identical; a reproduction, replica
   ANTONYM: an original

It was a fad in the 1960s to test the **capacity** (word 3) of little cars by seeing how many people could fit inside them.

7. **keen**
(kēn)

(adj.) having a sharpened edge; quick and sharp in thought or in sight, hearing, or smell; eager

Birds of prey have _____**keen**_____ *eyesight.*

SYNONYMS: razor-edged; acute, alert; eager, ready
ANTONYMS: dull, blunt; lazy, unwilling

8. **provoke**
(prə 'vōk)

(v.) to annoy or make angry, stir up; to do something in order to get a response

Name-calling is bound to _____**provoke**_____ *an argument.*

SYNONYMS: to excite, enrage, madden, goad
ANTONYMS: to calm, soothe, pacify, quiet

9. **spurt**
(spərt)

(v.) to shoot out quickly in a stream; to show a burst of energy

We watched the runners _____**spurt**_____ *for the finish line.*

(n.) a sudden, short stream of fluid; a quick burst of activity

My shirt was stained by a _____**spurt**_____ *of ketchup.*

SYNONYMS: to squirt, gush, flow; a jet, surge

10. **undoing**
(ən 'dü iŋ)

(n.) a bringing to ruin or destruction; the cause of ruin; unfastening or loosening

Idle gossip was the cause of their _____**undoing**_____.

SYNONYMS: downfall, misfortune, trouble; an opening
ANTONYMS: good luck, fortune, success; fastening

11. **vast**
(vast)

(adj.) very great or very large

A _____**vast**_____ *desert stretched into the distance.*

SYNONYMS: huge, enormous, spacious
ANTONYMS: tiny, small, little, narrow

12. **withdraw**
(with 'drô)

(v.) to pull out or remove; to move back or away, retreat

Is it too late to _____**withdraw**_____ *from the race?*

SYNONYMS: to subtract; to leave, depart, retreat
ANTONYMS: to deposit, enter; to attack

Match the Meaning

For each item choose the word whose meaning is suggested by the clue given. Then write the word in the space provided.

1. Your teacher might use a copier to _____**duplicate**_____ an assignment.
   a. provoke   b. duplicate   c. accomplish   d. spurt

2. A person who is not part of the military is a(n) _____**civilian**_____.
   a. civilian   b. capacity   c. spurt   d. undoing

3. To remove something is to _____**withdraw**_____ it.
   a. provoke   b. conceal   c. withdraw   d. duplicate

4. The number of people who can fit into a room depends upon its _____**capacity**_____.
   a. capacity   b. spurts   c. duplicates   d. civilians

5. Something that seems obvious is said to be _____**apparent**_____.
   a. keen   b. vast   c. apparent   d. civilian

6. A(n) _____**spurt**_____ from a garden hose might get you wet.
   a. undoing   b. duplicate   c. spurt   d. capacity

7. A(n) _____**keen**_____ blade will cut much better than a dull one.
   a. keen   b. apparent   c. vast   d. civilian

8. If you tease someone, you might _____**provoke**_____ that person.
   a. accomplish   b. conceal   c. provoke   d. withdraw

9. A serious mistake might lead to one's _____**undoing**_____.
   a. capacity   b. spurt   c. civilian   d. undoing

10. To hide something is to _____**conceal**_____ it.
    a. accomplish   b. conceal   c. provoke   d. withdraw

11. The Atlantic Ocean is a(n) _____**vast**_____ body of water.
    a. keen   b. duplicate   c. apparent   d. vast

12. When you reach your goal, you have _____**accomplished**_____ something.
    a. concealed   b. withdrawn   c. duplicated   d. accomplished

Synonyms

*For each item below choose the word that is most nearly the **same** in meaning as the word or phrase in **boldface**. Then write your choice on the line provided.*

1. create an **identical** set of plans
   a. vast   b. duplicate   c. keen   d. apparent   _duplicate_

2. measured the trunk's **room**
   a. capacity   b. spurt   c. civilian   d. undoing   _capacity_

3. **complete** the mission in two weeks
   a. provoke   b. duplicate   c. accomplish   d. withdraw   _accomplish_

4. led to the **downfall** of the dictator
   a. civilian   b. spurt   c. capacity   d. undoing   _undoing_

5. **depart** from the battlefield
   a. withdraw   b. provoke   c. spurt   d. conceal   _withdraw_

6. water that **squirted** from the hose
   a. concealed   b. spurted   c. withdrew   d. provoked   _spurted_

Antonyms

*For each item below choose the word that is most nearly **opposite** in meaning to the word or phrase in **boldface**. Then write your choice on the line provided.*

1. a **hidden** reason
   a. apparent   b. keen   c. civilian   d. vast   _apparent_

2. a **military** operation
   a. apparent   b. civilian   c. keen   d. vast   _civilian_

3. a **small** field
   a. keen   b. duplicate   c. civilian   d. vast   _vast_

4. **calm** the animal
   a. provoke   b. conceal   c. duplicate   d. accomplish   _provoke_

5. **reveal** the answers
   a. duplicate   b. provoke   c. conceal   d. withdraw   _conceal_

6. a **dull** sense of humor
   a. vast   b. civilian   c. duplicate   d. keen   _keen_

Completing the Sentence

From the list of words on pages 48–49, choose the one that best completes each item below. Then write the word in the space provided. (You may have to change the word's ending.)

REVOLUTION IN AMERICA AND FRANCE

■ One of the events that led to the American Revolution was the Boston Massacre, when British soldiers fired into a crowd of _____**civilians**_____.

■ Some historians say that the soldiers were _____**provoked**_____ into firing by the insults and taunts of the crowd.

■ It soon became _____**apparent**_____ to the British—even those who preferred not to see it—that the American colonies would settle for nothing less than full independence.

■ The leaders of the French Revolution were inspired by the American Revolution and hoped to _____**duplicate**_____ its success.

■ The Revolution in France led to the death of King Louis and the _____**undoing**_____ of the old order.

A CALIFORNIA DESERT

■ With an area of 25,000 square miles, the Mojave Desert covers a(n) _____**vast**_____ area of southern California. On the desert's border is Death Valley, the lowest point in North America.

■ During the daytime some animals, like the kangaroo rat, _____**withdraw**_____ from the hot desert floor to cooler underground burrows.

■ Though the desert roadrunner is a poor flier, it can run in quick _____**spurts**_____ to capture its prey. The roadrunner feeds on lizards, snakes, and insects.

THE SIXTEENTH PRESIDENT

■ In his _____**capacity**_____ as commander in chief, Abraham Lincoln played an important part in choosing the generals of the Union armies.

■ One of Lincoln's choices was Ulysses S. Grant, who _____**accomplished**_____ what no other Union general before him had been able to do—force the surrender of Robert E. Lee.

■ Lincoln's aides so feared for his safety that they often went to great lengths to _____**conceal**_____ his movements.

■ The many examples of his jokes and stories show that Lincoln possessed a(n) _____**keen**_____ sense of humor.

Word Associations

*Circle the letter next to the word or expression that best completes the sentence or answers the question. Pay special attention to the word in **boldface**.*

1. To **duplicate** a recipe, you might
   a. change it
   b. copy it
   c. memorize it
   d. hide it

2. When you **provoke** someone, that person is likely
   a. to thank you
   b. to forget you
   c. to be angry with you
   d. to praise you

3. Which is a **vast** distance?
   a. between Earth and Mars
   b. between your ears
   c. between footsteps
   d. between telephone poles

4. To **accomplish** something, you must
   a. think negative thoughts
   b. have lunch
   c. start at the beginning
   d. forget about it

5. You might **conceal** yourself
   a. in a chair
   b. on a busy sidewalk
   c. in a closet
   d. on top of your desk

6. Which is *not* a **civilian**?
   a. a teacher
   b. a lawyer
   c. a police officer
   d. a plumber

7. If you feel a **spurt** of energy, you
   a. might run faster
   b. might take a nap
   c. might go to the doctor
   d. might take a vitamin

8. People who have **keen** hearing
   a. can barely hear a loud siren
   b. need to have their ears examined
   c. would talk loudly
   d. can hear a pin drop

9. One of the things about you that is most **apparent** is
   a. your birthday
   b. the number of siblings you have
   c. the color of your hair
   d. whether or not you have a pet

10. You might measure the **capacity** of
    a. a bathtub
    b. a shower curtain
    c. a bar of soap
    d. a bath mat

11. Which might be a diet's **undoing**?
    a. lots of willpower
    b. lots of exercise
    c. lack of desserts
    d. lack of willpower

12. When a turtle **withdraws** its head, it
    a. wants you to pet its head
    b. pulls its head into its shell
    c. stretches its neck
    d. is ready to race

Definitions

Study the spelling, pronunciation, part of speech, and definition given for each of the words below. Write the word in the blank space in the sentence that follows. Then read the synonyms and antonyms.

1. **barrier**
   ('bar ē ər)

   (n.) something that blocks the way; an obstacle
   Volunteers worked feverishly to build _____ barriers _____ that would keep the forest fire from spreading.

   SYNONYMS: an obstruction, fence, wall, blockade, safeguard
   ANTONYMS: an opening, passage

2. **calculate**
   ('kal kyə lāt)

   (v.) to find out by using mathematics, reckon; to find out by reasoning, estimate
   The math teacher asked us to _____ calculate _____ the number of hours we spend on homework each week.

   SYNONYMS: to gauge, figure, determine, judge

3. **compose**
   (kəm 'pōz)

   (v.) to be or make up the parts of, form; to create or write; to calm or quiet one's mind
   Before you _____ compose _____ the essay, you might write an outline.

   SYNONYMS: to produce, invent; to still, settle
   ANTONYMS: to annoy, disturb

4. **considerable**
   (kən 'sid ər ə bəl)

   (adj.) fairly large in size or extent; worthy of attention
   It will take a _____ considerable _____ amount of time to complete the science project.

   SYNONYMS: great, sizable, major, important
   ANTONYMS: small, slight, negligible

5. **deputy**
   ('de pyə tē)

   (n.) one chosen to help or take the place of another or to act in that person's absence
   The sheriff's first act after winning the election was to appoint a _____ deputy _____.

   SYNONYMS: an assistant, aide, substitute

6. **industrious**
   (in 'dəs trē əs)

   (adj.) busy, working steadily
   The crew that gathered to clean up the vacant lot were as _____ industrious _____ as ants.

   SYNONYMS: active, occupied, energetic, untiring
   ANTONYMS: lazy, idle, loafing, slow

A dam is a man-made **barrier** (word 1) constructed to control the flow of water. The dam shown here is the Kariba in the African nation of Zimbabwe.

7. **jolt**
   (jōlt)

(v.) to shake up roughly; to move along in a jerky or bumpy fashion
It was fun to _____jolt_____ down the dirt road in the wagon.

(n.) a sudden bump or jerk; a shock or surprise
We felt a _____jolt_____ as the Ferris wheel started.

SYNONYMS: to jar, rattle, hit; a lurch, bounce

8. **loot**
   (lüt)

(v.) to rob by force or violence, especially during war or time of unrest
The soldiers were warned not to _____loot_____ the villages.

(n.) valuable things that have been stolen or taken by force
Detectives found _____loot_____ from a dozen robberies.

SYNONYMS: to steal, plunder; booty, prize, spoils

9. **rejoice**
   (ri 'jois)

(v.) to feel joy or great delight; to make joyful
The whole town will _____rejoice_____ if the team wins the championship.

SYNONYMS: to celebrate, cheer
ANTONYMS: to grieve, mourn

10. **reliable**
    (re 'lī ə bəl)

(adj.) deserving trust, dependable
It is not easy to find a _____reliable_____ babysitter.

SYNONYMS: faithful, proven, trustworthy
ANTONYMS: unreliable, questionable, fickle

11. **senseless**
    ('sens ləs)

(adj.) lacking meaning, stupid or foolish; without use of the senses
The boxer was knocked _____senseless_____ by the blow.

SYNONYMS: ridiculous, silly, illogical, birdbrained; unconscious
ANTONYMS: brilliant, clever, smart

12. **shrivel**
    ('shriv əl)

(v.) to shrink and wrinkle, especially from heat, cold or dryness
Exposed skin will _____shrivel_____ in the frosty air.

SYNONYMS: to wither, dry, contract
ANTONYMS: to expand, enlarge, swell

Match the Meaning

For each item below choose the word whose meaning is suggested by the clue given. Then write the word in the space provided.

1. _____Industrious_____ people always stay busy finding things to do.
   a. considerable   b. senseless   c. reliable   d. industrious

2. Because we forgot to water the plants, they all _____shriveled_____.
   a. composed   b. shriveled   c. calculated   d. rejoiced

3. When I ride my bike on an unpaved road, I feel a _____jolt_____ with each bump.
   a. jolt   b. barrier   c. deputy   d. loot

4. An action without meaning may be called _____senseless_____.
   a. industrious   b. considerable   c. senseless   d. reliable

5. Something that poses an obstacle is called a _____barrier_____.
   a. jolt   b. deputy   c. loot   d. barrier

6. Add the cost of all the food and drinks, as well as the tax and tip, to
   _____calculate_____ the total cost of the meal.
   a. jolt   b. calculate   c. rejoice   d. compose

7. A person chosen to act in another's absence is a _____deputy_____.
   a. deputy   b. loot   c. jolt   d. barrier

8. Calm yourself and quiet your mind to _____compose_____ your thoughts.
   a. calculate   b. rejoice   c. compose   d. jolt

9. A _____considerable_____ number is a pretty large one.
   a. reliable   b. industrious   c. considerable   d. senseless

10. A(n) _____reliable_____ car starts up every morning, even in winter.
    a. industrious   b. senseless   c. considerable   d. reliable

11. To celebrate with delight is to _____rejoice_____.
    a. shrivel   b. rejoice   c. calculate   d. compose

12. The robbers stashed their _____loot_____ in an old refrigerator.
    a. loot   b. barrier   c. deputy   d. jolt

Synonyms

*For each item below choose the word that is most nearly the **same** in meaning as the word or phrase in **boldface**. Then write your choice on the line provided.*

1. knocked **unconscious** when I fell off the ladder
   a. industrious   b. senseless   c. considerable d. reliable   _____ senseless

2. **jarred** by the rough landing
   a. jolted   b. composed   c. shriveled   d. looted   _____ jolted

3. **produce** a long poem
   a. jolt   b. calculate   c. compose   d. rejoice   _____ compose

4. played the **assistant**
   a. barrier   b. loot   c. deputy   d. jolt   _____ deputy

5. **determine** the cost of painting the apartment
   a. compose   b. rejoice   c. jolt   d. calculate   _____ calculate

6. to **plunder** the house while the owners were away
   a. jolt   b. compose   c. loot   d. calculate   _____ loot

Antonyms

*For each item below choose the word that is most nearly **opposite** in meaning to the word or phrase in **boldface**. Then write your choice on the line provided.*

1. an **idle** carpenter
   a. considerable b. industrious   c. reliable   d. senseless   _____ industrious

2. **swell** in the heat
   a. calculate   b. jolt   c. compose   d. shrivel   _____ shrivel

3. **mourn** over the election results
   a. loot   b. calculate   c. rejoice   d. shrivel   _____ rejoice

4. made a **slight** difference
   a. considerable b. industrious   c. senseless   d. reliable   _____ considerable

5. a **questionable** source of information
   a. industrious   b. considerable c. reliable   d. senseless   _____ reliable

6. found an **opening**
   a. deputy   b. loot   c. jolt   d. barrier   _____ barrier

Completing the Sentence

From the list of words on pages 54–55, choose the one that best completes each item below. Then write the word in the space provided. (You may have to change the word's ending.)

EARTHQUAKE!

■ The powerful earthquake that hit the San Francisco Bay area on October 17, 1989, did _____considerable_____ damage to the city, though not nearly so much as was done by the terrible earthquake and fire of 1906.

■ The mighty _____jolt_____, which registered 7.1 on the Richter scale, shook buildings and buckled elevated highways.

■ Safety officials quickly put up _____barriers_____ to keep people away from unsafe areas.

■ Scientists _____calculated_____ that the loss of life and property would have been far greater if the earthquake had hit during the day instead of early evening.

A GREAT ARTIST

■ The Dutch painter Vincent van Gogh was an ambitious and _____industrious_____ artist who made hundreds of paintings and drawings during his short lifetime. He moved to southern France in 1888, and there he produced many of his masterpieces. Van Gogh died in 1890 at the age of 37.

■ Van Gogh _____rejoiced_____ at the completion of each new painting, but despaired that his work never sold.

■ As the summer heat _____shriveled_____ the olives on the trees near his home, van Gogh wrote sad letters to his brother Theo.

■ He _____composed_____ works of great beauty that were not appreciated until after his death. Today his paintings are in museums all over the world and are sold for millions of dollars.

SIRENS IN THE NIGHT

■ When a power blackout darkened part of the city, some criminals roamed the streets. They broke windows and _____looted_____ neighborhood stores.

■ Community leaders spoke out against this _____senseless_____ violence and urged people to act responsibly during the emergency.

■ Several sheriff's _____deputies_____ arrived to restore order and interview witnesses to the crime spree.

■ One witness offered information about the robberies, but the police officers paid him little mind because they knew he was not _____reliable_____.

Circle the letter next to the word or expression that best completes the sentence or answers the question. Pay special attention to the word in **boldface.**

1. Which is a **barrier** to success in school?
   a. poor study habits
   b. weak stomach muscles
   c. a tall fence
   d. no brothers or sisters

2. An **industrious** person could
   a. build a hen house in ten years
   b. build a doll house in five years
   c. build a birdhouse in one year
   d. build a doghouse in one day

3. A **deputy** would probably carry
   a. a badge
   b. a bag lunch
   c. a wrench
   d. a banner

4. It is **senseless** to try to count
   a. to one thousand
   b. change after a purchase
   c. grains of sand at the beach
   d. people ahead of you in line

5. You might **rejoice** if you
   a. found your lost dog
   b. ruined your favorite shirt
   c. failed a spelling test
   d. saw the latest comedy film

6. Which is a **considerable** sum?
   a. 30¢
   b. $1.00
   c. $5.00
   d. $5,000.00

7. If you **compose** your autobiography, you will be
   a. driving a new car
   b. writing the story of your life
   c. interviewing strangers
   d. making up a new song

8. You might feel **jolted** by
   a. a good night's sleep
   b. a delicious lunch
   c. shocking news
   d. yesterday's paper

9. People guilty of **looting** are
   a. winning a prize
   b. breaking the law
   c. running in circles
   d. taking pictures

10. A balloon would quickly **shrivel**
    a. if air leaks from it
    b. if it floats away
    c. if it gets wet
    d. if it is tied to a string

11. A **reliable** friend is one who
    a. doesn't let you down
    b. makes fun of you
    c. is never on time
    d. always makes you laugh

12. Which might be used to **calculate**?
    a. an alarm clock
    b. paper and pencil
    c. a hammer
    d. knife and fork

Definitions

Study the spelling, pronunciation, part of speech, and definition given for each of the words below. Write the word in the blank space in the sentence that follows. Then read the synonyms and antonyms.

1. **alternate**
   (*v.*, 'ôl tər nāt;
   n., *adj.*, 'ôl tər nət)

   (v.) to do, use, or happen in successive turns; to take turns
   > *We chose two students to* _____ **alternate** _____ *in the lead roles for our class play.*

   (n.) a person acting or prepared to act in place of another; a substitute
   > *Juries usually include two or more* _____ **alternates** _____ .

   (adj.) happening or appearing in turns; every other; being a choice between two or more things
   > *The bus driver took an* _____ **alternate** _____ *route.*

   SYNONYMS: to rotate, change; a replacement, deputy

2. **demolish**
   (di 'mäl ish)

   (v.) to tear down, break to pieces
   > *A wrecking crew arrived to* _____ **demolish** _____ *the old building.*

   SYNONYMS: to raze, destroy, wreck, smash, level
   ANTONYMS: to construct, build, restore, mend

3. **energetic**
   (e nər 'je tik)

   (adj.) active and vigorous, full of energy, forceful
   > *Our teacher has an* _____ **energetic** _____ *assistant.*

   SYNONYMS: hardworking, tireless, peppy
   ANTONYMS: idle, lazy, inactive

4. **enforce**
   (in 'fôrs)

   (v.) to force obedience to
   > *It is the duty of the police to protect citizens and* _____ **enforce** _____ *the laws.*

   SYNONYM: to carry out
   ANTONYMS: to overlook, abandon, disregard

5. **feat**
   (fēt)

   (n.) an act or deed that shows daring, skill, or strength
   > *The crowd cheered when the circus strongman performed a mighty* _____ **feat** _____ .

   SYNONYMS: an achievement, exploit, effort, stroke

6. **hearty**
   ('härt ē)

   (adj.) warm and friendly; healthy, lively, and strong; large and satisfying to the appetite
   > *We all sat down to enjoy a* _____ **hearty** _____ *meal.*

   SYNONYMS: cheerful, friendly; fit, healthy; plentiful
   ANTONYMS: insincere, phony; weak, sickly

Sometimes explosives are used to **demolish** (word 2) structures. Here an old hotel is brought down in Atlantic City, New Jersey.

7. **mature**
   (mə 'tǔr)

(v.) to bring to or reach full development or growth
The puppy will _____mature_____ over the summer.
(adj.) fully grown or developed
A field of _____mature_____ oats waved in the breeze.

SYNONYMS: to grow, develop, age, ripen; complete, ripe
ANTONYMS: immature, inexperienced, raw, green

8. **observant**
   (əb 'zər vənt)

(adj.) watchful, quick to notice; careful and diligent
An _____observant_____ guard spotted the vandals.

SYNONYMS: aware, attentive, alert, sharp; dutiful, mindful
ANTONYMS: inattentive, careless

9. **primary**
   ('prī mer ē)

(adj.) first in importance, first in time or order; basic, fundamental
Raising money was our _____primary_____ order of business.
(n.) an early election that narrows the choice of candidates who will run in a final election
The challenger won the _____primary_____.

SYNONYMS: highest, main, prime
ANTONYMS: secondary, last

10. **resign**
    (ri 'zīn)

(v.) to give up a job, office, or a right or claim
Richard Nixon was the first President to _____resign_____ the office.

SYNONYMS: to quit, abandon, leave, surrender

11. **strive**
    (strīv)

(v.) to devote much energy or effort, try hard
You must _____strive_____ to finish your homework in time.

SYNONYMS: to attempt, struggle, labor, slave, strain

12. **verdict**
    ('vər dikt)

(n.) the decision of a jury at the end of a trial or legal case; any decision
The jury brought in a guilty _____verdict_____.

SYNONYMS: a ruling, judgment, finding

Match the Meaning

For each item below choose the word whose meaning is suggested by the clue given. Then write the word in the space provided.

1. To make people obey laws is to _____enforce_____ those laws.
   a. enforce   b. alternate   c. demolish   d. strive

2. To break something to pieces is to _____demolish_____ it.
   a. alternate   b. demolish   c. resign   d. mature

3. An amazing act or deed might be called a(n) _____feat_____.
   a. feat   b. verdict   c. primary   d. alternate

4. On cold mornings, my favorite breakfast is a(n) _____hearty_____ bowl of hot oatmeal with brown sugar, cinnamon, and walnuts.
   a. mature   b. observant   c. hearty   d. primary

5. The decision that a jury gives at the end of a trial is called the _____verdict_____.
   a. feat   b. primary   c. alternate   d. verdict

6. If you give up a job, you _____resign_____ from it.
   a. enforce   b. resign   c. mature   d. alternate

7. Something that is first in importance, first in time order, or first in another basic way is called _____primary_____.
   a. primary   b. mature   c. alternate   d. energetic

8. In most games, players take turns or _____alternate_____ moves.
   a. resign   b. demolish   c. alternate   d. enforce

9. A frisky puppy can be described as _____energetic_____.
   a. observant   b. energetic   c. mature   d. primary

10. If you are very _____observant_____, you'll notice the clues.
    a. primary   b. hearty   c. mature   d. observant

11. Once fruit is fully _____mature_____, it can be harvested.
    a. demolish   b. mature   c. resign   d. alternate

12. To try very hard is to _____strive_____.
    a. strive   b. alternate   c. demolish   d. resign

Synonyms

*For each item below choose the word that is most nearly the **same** in meaning as the word or phrase in **boldface**. Then write your choice on the line provided.*

1. handed down the **ruling**
   a. primary   b. feat   c. alternate   d. verdict   _____ verdict

2. a **cheerful** laugh that made his shoulders jiggle
   a. alternate   b. hearty   c. mature   d. observant   _____ hearty

3. read about the daring **achievement**
   a. feat   b. verdict   c. primary   d. alternate   _____ feat

4. packed a **replacement** camera as a back-up
   a. feat   b. verdict   c. primary   d. alternate   _____ alternate

5. **abandon** the job of manager
   a. alternate   b. demolish   c. strive   d. resign   _____ resign

6. **attempt** to learn to read Japanese
   a. demolish   b. alternate   c. strive   d. resign   _____ strive

Antonyms

*For each item below choose the word that is most nearly **opposite** in meaning to the word or phrase in **boldface**. Then write your choice on the line provided.*

1. **construct** a covered bridge
   a. demolish   b. strive   c. alternate   d. enforce   _____ demolish

2. **idle** workers
   a. mature   b. energetic   c. observant   d. primary   _____ energetic

3. showed an **inexperienced** outlook
   a. alternate   b. hearty   c. mature   d. primary   _____ mature

4. an **inattentive** reader
   a. alternate   b. mature   c. observant   d. hearty   _____ observant

5. **overlook** the "No Smoking" laws
   a. alternate   b. strive   c. resign   d. enforce   _____ enforce

6. a **secondary** cause of blindness
   a. hearty   b. observant   c. primary   d. energetic   _____ primary

Completing the Sentence

From the list of words on pages 60–61, choose the one that best completes each item below. Write the word in the space provided. (You may have to change the word's ending.)

RAISING A NEW HOUSE

■ The storm so badly damaged the house that it was unsafe to live in. The owner decided to _____ **demolish** _____ it and build a new one.

■ It was quite a(n) _____ **feat** _____ to tear down the house, clear the land, and build another house in only ten weeks!

■ Two crews _____ **alternated** _____ in the building work. When one finished, the other began, so that construction went on from break of day until long after the sun went down.

■ All of the workers were encouraged to _____ **strive** _____ as hard as they could to finish the job ahead of schedule.

■ Luckily, a(n) _____ **observant** _____ worker spotted a mistake in the building plans before it caused a delay, and the house was finished on time. The worker was rewarded for his attention and diligence.

AN AFTER-SCHOOL JOB

■ My sister says that the responsibilities of a part-time job can help teens develop into more _____ **mature** _____ individuals.

■ The managers at Burger Barn, where she works after school, _____ **enforce** _____ three rules: be on time, be honest, and be polite.

■ As long as she follows those rules, the managers greet her each day with a cheerful smile and a _____ **hearty** _____ handshake.

TO THE POLLS!

■ The _____ **primary** _____ election in September decided which candidates would run for state assembly in the general election in November. In the Democratic race, two politicians challenged the two-term assemblyman for a place on the ballot.

■ All three candidates had the help of many young, _____ **energetic** _____ volunteers, who worked tirelessly to get out the vote.

■ After ballots were counted, the _____ **verdict** _____ was clear: Voters wanted the two-term assemblyman to run again.

■ However, health problems in October forced him to _____ **resign** _____ his office and pull out of the election.

*Circle the letter next to the word or expression that best completes the sentence or answers the question. Pay special attention to the word in **boldface**.*

1. Which is a **verdict**?
   a. "Thank you!"
   b. "Good morning!"
   c. "I told you so!"
   d. "Not guilty!"

2. If you and your sister **alternate** walking the dog, then you must
   a. do twice as much walking
   b. walk the dog every other time
   c. get another dog
   d. wear the collar and leash

3. Which is a firefighter's **feat**?
   a. polishing the fire trucks
   b. making daring rescues
   c. wearing waterproof boots
   d. cooking firehouse stew

4. Who would **enforce** a leash law?
   a. a scientist
   b. a weather forecaster
   c. a veterinarian
   d. a dogcatcher

5. People who **strive**
   a. give up easily
   b. always succeed
   c. do their very best
   d. prefer to be outdoors

6. Which is a **mature** animal?
   a. a quick tadpole
   b. an old turtle
   c. a frisky kitten
   d. a new chick

7. An **energetic** performer might
   a. do three shows a day
   b. nap during intermission
   c. not answer fan mail
   d. sing softly

8. Which might be **resigned**?
   a. a greeting card
   b. a doctor's prescription
   c. a homework assignment
   d. a club membership

9. A **primary** concern is one that
   a. comes last
   b. comes too late
   c. comes first
   d. comes when you least expect it

10. Which might be **hearty**?
    a. a wink
    b. a laugh
    c. a sigh
    d. a whisper

11. If you are **observant,** you are
    a. wide awake
    b. daydreaming
    c. asleep
    d. distracted

12. Which would be the hardest to **demolish**?
    a. a snow fort
    b. a house made of cards
    c. a skyscraper
    d. a dollhouse

Selecting Word Meanings

*For each of the following items circle the choice that is most nearly the **same** in meaning as the word in **boldface**.*

1. asked him to **resign**
   a. accept   (b.) quit   c. join   d. stay

2. discovered the pirates' **loot**
   a. bones   b. weapons   c. gifts   (d.) stolen goods

3. **senseless** behavior
   (a.) foolish   b. polite   c. noble   d. unusual

4. welcomed the **nomads**
   a. workers   b. guests   c. relatives   (d.) wanderers

5. an **energetic** group
   a. lazy   (b.) lively   c. quiet   d. friendly

6. **calculate** the distance traveled
   (a.) figure   b. walk   c. question   d. write down

7. a courageous **feat**
   a. failure   b. battle   c. idea   (d.) deed

8. the **supreme** example
   (a.) outstanding   b. original   c. unimportant   d. personal

9. **concealed** my fears
   (a.) hid   b. showed   c. emphasized   d. ignored

10. explored the **vast** continent
    a. beautiful   b. frozen   c. empty   (d.) huge

11. **detected** by radar
    a. hidden   b. decided   (c.) discovered   d. photographed

12. wore **civilian** clothes
    a. new   b. military   c. party   (d.) non-military

Spelling

*For each item below study the **boldface** word in which there is a blank. If a letter is missing, fill in the blank to make a correctly spelled word. If the word is already spelled correctly, leave the blank empty.*

1. a **verdi_c_t** of not guilty

2. **jo___lted** by the earthquake

3. an **industri_o_us** effort

4. the aquarium's **capa_c_ity**

5. ask the **depu_t_y** mayor

6. **he___arty** applause

7. **enfor_c_e** the regulations

8. keep the **d_u_plicate**

9. an **ap_p_arent** mistake

10. the **festi_v_e** mood

11. the family's **hos___pitality**

12. **ac_c_omplish** a great deal

Antonyms

*For each of the following items circle the choice that is most nearly the **opposite** in meaning to the word in **boldface**.*

1. arrived at the **barrier**
   a. passage   b. obstacle   c. river   d. corner

2. a knife's **keen** edge
   a. sharp   b. rusty   c. dull   d. broken

3. **demolished** the car
   a. built   b. destroyed   c. sold   d. washed

4. showed signs of **fatigue**
   a. surprise   b. exhaustion   c. sickness   d. energy

5. a **considerable** collection of coins
   a. small   b. huge   c. valuable   d. private

6. the **spurting** water fountain
   a. gushing   b. brand-new   c. trickling   d. old

7. the writer's **primary** meaning
   a. main   b. hidden   c. secondary   d. confusing

8. **persecuted** by their neighbors
   a. hurt   b. comforted   c. questioned   d. ignored

Words have been left out of the following passage. For each numbered item in the passage, fill in the circle next to the word in the margin that best fills the blank space. Then answer each question below by writing a sentence that contains one of the words you have chosen.

Elizabeth Blackwell wanted to be a doctor. Unfortunately, in the mid-1800s no medical schools accepted women students. Many people at the time thought that women would not make __1__ doctors. But Elizabeth did not give up her dream.

She applied to medical schools but was turned down over and over again. Still Elizabeth persisted. She continued to apply to medical schools, but she also came up with a(n) __2__ means of receiving an education in medicine. She read medical books on her own and later convinced a doctor to teach her privately.

Finally, in 1847, a small school in New York State admitted her. When she arrived, Elizabeth found out that she had been admitted as a joke. But she did not allow this disappointment to keep her from __3__ her goal. She stood her ground and was allowed to attend classes.

Two years later, Elizabeth Blackwell graduated at the head of the class. In 1857 she succeeded in establishing the New York Infirmary. Elizabeth Blackwell's pioneering efforts helped to break down the __4__ against other women who wanted careers in medicine.

1. ○ duplicate
   ○ primary
   ○ considerable
   ● capable

2. ○ festive
   ○ vast
   ● alternate
   ○ energetic

3. ○ concealing
   ○ resigning
   ● accomplishing
   ○ enforcing

4. ○ deputies
   ○ verdicts
   ○ civilians
   ● barriers

5. How did Elizabeth Blackwell's efforts help other women?

   Her efforts helped break down the **barriers** that kept women out of the medical profession.

6. Why were women not accepted to medical school in the mid-1800s?

   Many people believed women were not **capable** of becoming doctors.

7. How did Elizabeth react when she found out that her acceptance was a joke?

   She did not allow her disappointment to keep her from **accomplishing** her goal.

8. What did Elizabeth Blackwell do while she continued to apply to medical schools?

   She found an **alternate** means of getting an education.

Analogies

In each of the following circle the letter for the item that best completes the comparison. Then explain the relationship on the lines provided.

1. **dependable** is to **reliable** as
   a. hearty is to sickly
   b. dry is to moist
   c. round is to circular
   d. logical is to senseless

   Relationship: "Dependable" and "reliable" are synonyms/mean the same; "round" and "circular" are synonyms/mean the same.

2. **begin** is to **conclude** as
   a. search is to look
   b. help is to aid
   c. remain is to stay
   d. give up is to strive

   Relationship: "Begin" and "conclude" are antonyms/opposite in meaning; "give up" and "strive" are antonyms/opposite in meaning.

3. **apparent** is to **obvious** as
   a. first is to primary
   b. dull is to keen
   c. early is to late
   d. mature is to immature

   Relationship: "Apparent" and "obvious" are synonyms/mean the same; "first" and "primary" are synonyms/mean the same.

4. **celebration** is to **rejoice** as
   a. library is to shout
   b. contest is to compete
   c. feast is to starve
   d. barn raising is to demolish

   Relationship: One would rejoice at a celebration; one would compete in a contest.

Challenge: Make up your own

Write a comparison using the words in the box below. (Hint: There are three possible analogies.) Then write the relationship on the lines provided. One comparison has been completed for you.

sword	blemish	barracks	club
civilian	home	soldier	barrier
flaw	blunt	keen	obstacle

Analogy: _____ is to _____ as _____ is to _____.

Relationship: See Table of Contents _____

Word Families

*The words in **boldface** in the sentences below are related to words introduced in Units 5–8. For example, the nouns festivity and energy in item 1 are related to the adjectives festive (Unit 5) and energetic (Unit 8). Based on your understanding of the unit words that follow, circle the related word in **boldface** that best completes each sentence.*

industrious	festive	detect	capable	calculate
compose	reliable	mature	observant	accomplish
transport	energetic	alternate	hospitality	supreme
undoing	duplicate	enforce	blunt	provoke

1. If you are going on a long hike over steep hills on a hot summer day, you will need a lot of (**festivity**/**energy**).

2. The Environmental Protection Agency is responsible for the (**enforcement**/**duplication**) of laws passed to ensure clean air and water for all Americans.

3. For English class I wrote a (**calculation**/**composition**) about my family's trip to the Grand Canyon.

4. Passengers on whale-watching cruises can (**observe**/**undo**) whales and sometimes dolphins swimming in the open ocean.

5. The guests at a party may talk about how (**provocative**/**hospitable**) their hosts are to everyone.

6. Today people can choose from many different kinds of (**transportation**/**detection**) to travel across the United States and around the world.

7. A computer has the (**capability**/**maturity**) to solve complicated mathematical problems very quickly.

8. Most bosses agree that (**bluntness**/**industry**) is a valuable quality in an employee.

9. My parents chose our new family car for its (**supremacy**/**reliability**) in all kinds of weather conditions.

10. All over the world people gather in front of television sets to watch the amazing (**accomplishments**/**alternatives**) of athletes at the Olympic Games.

Word Games

Go for the Gold! Find and ring the words from Units 5–8 that are hidden in the grid below. Then choose from these words the ones that best complete the sentences that follow. Write the words in the blanks.

S	R	E	L	I	A	B	L	E	N
T	O	P	O	S	B	L	E	M	O
R	C	C	O	N	C	E	A	L	M
I	K	O	T	K	I	M	S	T	A
V	E	N	V	L	U	I	E	A	D
E	T	C	R	O	V	S	B	W	E
A	L	L	W	N	Y	H	E	R	O
S	P	U	R	T	V	O	T	E	R
Z	O	D	U	O	F	F	E	A	T
K	E	E	N	N	D	G	Q	T	O

Countries from every continent send their finest and most _____**reliable**_____ athletes to compete in the Olympic Games.

All the athletes who take part in the games _____**strive**_____ to do their very best for their countries, their teams, and themselves.

People all over the world watch the games with _____**keen**_____ interest.

Some athletes achieve the remarkable _____**feat**_____ of setting new world records.

Many athletes, such as speed skaters and marathon runners, may rely on an extra _____**spurt**_____ of energy at the finish of their races.

By tradition, the marathon is run on the day that the Games _____**conclude**_____.

Definitions

Choose the word from the box that matches each definition. Write the word on the line provided. The first one has been done for you.

alternate	apparent	barrier	blemish	blunder
capable	considerable	duplicate	feat	glamour
impressive	luxurious	miniature	persecute	solitary
scuffle	straggle	~~transport~~	undoing	verdict

1. to move or carry from one place to another   <u>transport</u>

2. a mark or stain that damages the appearance   <u>blemish</u>

3. fairly large in size or extent   <u>considerable</u>

4. to stray off or trail behind   <u>straggle</u>

5. living or being alone; being the only one   <u>solitary</u>

6. mysterious charm, beauty, or attractiveness   <u>glamour</u>

7. having a strong effect, commanding attention   <u>impressive</u>

8. a bringing to ruin; the cause of ruin   <u>undoing</u>

9. to copy exactly; to produce something equal to   <u>duplicate</u>

10. to make a foolish or careless mistake   <u>blunder</u>

11. the decision of a jury at the end of a trial   <u>verdict</u>

12. to take turns   <u>alternate</u>

13. able and prepared to do something; fit or skilled   <u>capable</u>

14. open to view; seeming to be true or real   <u>apparent</u>

15. a very small copy, model, or painting   <u>miniature</u>

Antonyms

*Choose the word from the box that is most nearly **opposite** in meaning to each group of words. Write the word on the line provided. The first one has been done for you.*

1. a rival, foe, enemy	associate	accomplish
2. sad, gloomy, somber	festive	aggressive
3. to accept, receive, take	reject	assault
4. inexperienced, raw, green	veteran	~~associate~~
5. to reveal, uncover	conceal	cautious
6. to grieve, mourn	rejoice	conceal
7. daring, reckless, wild	cautious	conclude
8. lasting, long-lived, permanent	temporary	despise
9. shy, bashful, retiring	aggressive	dispute
10. to begin, start, open	conclude	energetic
11. a hero, heroine, champion	villain	festive
12. idle, lazy, inactive	energetic	fragile
13. to defend, protect, resist	assault	haven
14. to hurry, rush, hasten	linger	justify
15. tiny, small, little	vast	linger
16. sturdy, hardy, strong	fragile	mature
17. to admire, esteem, adore	despise	reject
18. to expand, enlarge, swell	shrivel	rejoice
19. faithful, trustworthy; safe	treacherous	senseless
20. to agree; an agreement	dispute	shrivel
		temporary
		treacherous
		vast
		veteran
		villain

Cumulative Review I ■ *73*

Completing the Sentence

Choose the word from the box that best completes each sentence below. Write the word in the space provided. The first one has been done for you.

Group A

blunt	civilian	emigrate	hearty
hospitality	industrious	~~myth~~	resign

1. I enjoyed reading the story of Demeter and Persephone, a Greek
   _____ **myth** _____ that explains summer and winter.

2. Are you familiar with Aesop's fable about the lazy grasshopper and the
   _____ **industrious** _____ ant?

3. My cousins in eastern Europe hope to _____ **emigrate** _____ to the United
   States and join the rest of the family here.

4. I wrote a note to thank you for your gracious _____ **hospitality** _____
   last weekend.

5. Let's give a(n) _____ **hearty** _____ welcome to our guests who have
   traveled so far to be with us!

Group B

cancel	compose	hazy	obstacle
reliable	strategy	vivid	withdraw

1. Before asking Mom to increase our allowance, we'll plan a(n)
   _____ **strategy** _____ that is sure to succeed.

2. After Dad painted the car a(n) _____ **vivid** _____ shade of green, it was
   easy to spot in a crowded parking lot.

3. I plan to pay you as soon as I _____ **withdraw** _____ the money from the
   bank.

4. I have only a(n) _____ **hazy** _____ idea of what I will do during
   summer vacation.

5. Let's work together to _____ **compose** _____ lyrics for a new school song.

Classifying — *Choose the word from the box that goes best with each group of words. Write the word in the space provided. Then explain what the words have in common. The first one has been done for you.*

capacity	~~continuous~~	convert	detect	flexible
loot	monarch	nomad	numerous	primary

1. ongoing, endless, _____continuous_____

   The words are synonyms.

2. _____convert_____, conversion, convertible

   The words belong to the same family.

3. some, a few, many, _____numerous_____

   The words describe amounts.

4. president, dictator, _____monarch_____

   The words name heads of government.

5. bendable, adjustable, _____flexible_____

   The words are synonyms.

6. _____detect_____, detective, detector

   The words belong to the same family.

7. tribe, camel, tent, _____nomad_____

   The words relate to a way of life.

8. length, weight, _____capacity_____

   The words name kinds of measurement.

9. boot, root, hoot, _____loot_____

   The words rhyme.

10. _____primary_____, middle, secondary

   The words describe levels of school.

Definitions

Study the spelling, pronunciation, part of speech, and definition given for each of the words below. Write the word in the blank space in the sentence that follows. Then read the synonyms and antonyms.

1. **brisk**
   (brisk)

   (adj.) energetic, lively, fast; cool and fresh
   The flag snapped and fluttered in the _____ **brisk** _____ *wind.*

   SYNONYMS: quick, active, peppy, refreshing, nippy
   ANTONYMS: slow, dull, sluggish

2. **cherish**
   ('cher ish)

   (v.) to feel or show great love for; to value highly; to take special care of
   Our freedom is something we should always safeguard and _____ **cherish** _____ .

   SYNONYMS: to love, treasure, hold dear, honor; to prize, preserve
   ANTONYMS: to hate, despise, dishonor; to neglect

3. **considerate**
   (kən 'si də rət)

   (adj.) showing concern for the needs or feelings of others
   If you are a _____ **considerate** _____ *guest, you might be invited back.*

   SYNONYMS: thoughtful, kind, giving, gracious
   ANTONYMS: thoughtless, self-centered, selfish

4. **displace**
   (dis 'plās)

   (v.) to force to move or flee; to move out of position
   Officials feared that the flood would _____ **displace** _____ *the villagers from their homes.*

   SYNONYMS: to uproot, expel, evict, dislodge
   ANTONYMS: to settle, plant, install

5. **downfall**
   ('daůn fôl)

   (n.) a sudden fall from power or position; a sudden and heavy snow or rain
   To this day, historians argue over what caused the Roman empire's _____ **downfall** _____ .

   SYNONYMS: collapse, ruin
   ANTONYMS: triumph, success

6. **estimate**
   (v., 'es tə māt;
   n., 'es tə mət)

   (v.) to form a rough judgment about the size, quantity, or value of something
   I would _____ **estimate** _____ *the number of people at the concert at about 15,000.*

   (n.) a rough calculation; a careful guess
   The mechanic gave us an _____ **estimate** _____ *for the cost of the repairs.*

   SYNONYMS: to figure, judge; a guess, calculation, opinion

Fraternal twins may not look very much alike. But twins who are **identical** (word 8), like those pictured here, are usually very hard to tell apart.

7. **humiliate**
(hyü 'mi lē āt)

(v.) to hurt someone's self-respect or pride
Our opponents accused us of trying to _____humiliate_____ *them by running up the score.*

SYNONYMS: to shame, disgrace, dishonor, embarrass
ANTONYMS: to honor, applaud, praise

8. **identical**
(ī 'den ti kəl)

(adj.) exactly the same, alike in every way
The twins liked to wear _____identical_____ *outfits.*

SYNONYMS: matching, alike
ANTONYMS: unlike, different, opposite

9. **improper**
(im 'prä pər)

(adj.) not correct; showing bad manners or taste
The principal reminded us that _____improper_____ *behavior is not acceptable.*

SYNONYMS: incorrect, wrong; impolite, unsuitable, rude
ANTONYMS: proper, right; appropriate, polite

10. **poll**
(pōl)

(n.) a collecting of votes; (*usually plural*) a place where voting takes place; a collecting of opinions
Where did you see the results of the _____poll_____?

(v.) to receive votes; to vote; to question people to collect opinions
We are going to _____poll_____ *fifth graders about their favorite movies.*

SYNONYMS: an election; a survey, tally; to interview, tally up

11. **soothe**
(süth)

(v.) to make calm; to ease pain or sorrow
A nurse tried to _____soothe_____ *the fussy child.*

SYNONYMS: to quiet, pacify; to comfort, relieve
ANTONYMS: to excite, upset; to hurt, worsen

12. **vicinity**
(və 'si nə tē)

(n.) the area near a place, the surrounding region
There is a park in the _____vicinity_____ *of our school.*

SYNONYMS: neighborhood, area, surroundings

77

Match the Meaning

For each item choose the word whose meaning is suggested by the clue given. Then write the word in the space provided.

1. Things that look exactly alike are said to be _____ identical _____.
   a. brisk   b. improper   c. identical   d. considerate

2. A heavy snowstorm would produce a(n) _____ downfall _____.
   a. estimate   b. poll   c. vicinity   d. downfall

3. To make a hurt less painful is to _____ soothe _____ it.
   a. soothe   b. humiliate   c. displace   d. cherish

4. A grocery store in your neighborhood is in the _____ vicinity _____ of your home.
   a. poll   b. vicinity   c. downfall   d. estimate

5. A cool, breezy morning might be described as _____ brisk _____.
   a. considerate   b. identical   c. improper   d. brisk

6. A person who is thoughtful of the feelings of others is said to be _____ considerate _____.
   a. considerate   b. improper   c. identical   d. brisk

7. To learn the opinions of consumers, you might _____ poll _____ them.
   a. downfall   b. poll   c. vicinity   d. estimate

8. To take special care of something is to _____ cherish _____ it.
   a. poll   b. estimate   c. displace   d. cherish

9. A rough calculation is also called a(n) _____ estimate _____.
   a. vicinity   b. downfall   c. estimate   d. poll

10. To move something aside is to _____ displace _____ it.
    a. estimate   b. displace   c. soothe   d. humiliate

11. Rude behavior might be criticized as _____ improper _____.
    a. brisk   b. improper   c. considerate   d. identical

12. To embarrass or disgrace someone is to _____ humiliate _____ that person.
    a. poll   b. soothe   c. cherish   d. humiliate

Synonyms

For each item below choose the word that is most nearly the **same** in meaning as the word or phrase in **boldface**. Then write your choice on the line provided.

1. **dislodged** by the earthquake
   a. cherished   b. displaced   c. polled   d. soothed   _displaced_

2. **embarrassed** by a failing grade
   a. cherished   b. soothed   c. humiliated   d. displaced   _humiliated_

3. **treasure** the memory of my first home run
   a. estimate   b. poll   c. cherish   d. humiliate   _cherish_

4. **survey** voters on their choice for senator
   a. soothe   b. estimate   c. poll   d. humiliate   _poll_

5. recommended a restaurant in the **area**
   a. downfall   b. vicinity   c. poll   d. estimate   _vicinity_

6. **judged** the distance to be thirty feet
   a. polled   b. estimated   c. cherished   d. humiliated   _estimated_

Antonyms

For each item below choose the word that is most nearly **opposite** in meaning to the word or phrase in **boldface**. Then write your choice on the line provided.

1. the general's **triumph**
   a. downfall   b. estimate   c. poll   d. vicinity   _downfall_

2. set a **slow** pace
   a. identical   b. brisk   c. improper   d. considerate   _brisk_

3. held **different** views
   a. improper   b. brisk   c. identical   d. considerate   _identical_

4. truly **thoughtless** behavior
   a. considerate   b. brisk   c. identical   d. improper   _considerate_

5. **worsened** the pain
   a. humiliated   b. estimated   c. polled   d. soothed   _soothed_

6. **correct** use of the word
   a. brisk   b. considerate   c. improper   d. identical   _improper_

Completing the Sentence

From the list of words on pages 76–77, choose the one that best completes each item below. Then write the word in the blank space provided. (You may have to change the word's ending.)

A POLITICAL CHARGE BACKFIRES

■ In a heated speech late in the campaign, the mayor's opponent accused her of the _____**improper**_____ use of public funds. The mayor immediately denied the charge, declaring that she had never personally profited from her office.

■ A local newspaper conducted a _____**poll**_____ of likely voters. The results showed that more than 75% of those surveyed did not believe the charge leveled against the mayor.

■ Rather than be _____**humiliated**_____ by what would almost certainly be a lopsided defeat, her opponent pulled out of the race. The mayor went on to win the election by a landslide.

THE BUFFALO TRAIL

■ Before they were forcibly _____**displaced**_____ by federal troops and European settlers, hundreds of thousands of Native Americans dwelled on the Great Plains. Among these tribes were the Blackfeet, Crows, and Sioux.

■ _____**Brisk**_____ autumn winds and deep winter snows made warm clothing and shelter essential to survival on the Great Plains. Some of these robes and the tents were made from buffalo hides.

■ Because they were so dependent upon the buffalo for food as well, many tribes never strayed very far from the _____**vicinity**_____ of the huge herds that grazed the prairie.

■ Experts _____**estimate**_____ that as many as 30 million buffalo once roamed the vast open stretches of the northern Plains.

■ The Great Plains tribes _____**cherished**_____ their traditions and way of life. To dishonor these customs was a serious offense.

■ The destruction of the buffalo herds in the late 1800s was one of the factors that led to the _____**downfall**_____ of these tribes.

A FRIEND'S GOOD TURN

■ I was very upset to learn that a friend planned to come to the party in a costume _____**identical**_____ to mine.

■ To _____**soothe**_____ my hurt feelings, she offered to wear a different costume instead.

■ It was very _____**considerate**_____ of her to do that for me, don't you think?

Word Associations

*Circle the letter next to the word or expression that best completes the sentence or answers the question. Pay special attention to the word in **boldface**.*

1. Which of the following would you use after a **downfall**?
   a. a watering can
   b. a rake
   c. a snow shovel
   d. a hoe

2. To be **humiliated** would make you
   a. feel happy
   b. feel intelligent
   c. feel confident
   d. feel ashamed

3. If you **cherish** your pets, you
   a. will take good care of them
   b. will forget them
   c. will mistreat them
   d. will sell them

4. Which could you easily **estimate**?
   a. the height of your desk
   b. the number of all numbers
   c. the distance to Pluto
   d. the cost of a jumbo jet

5. Which can be **identical**?
   a. snowflakes
   b. twins
   c. fingerprints
   d. planets

6. What does one do at the **polls**?
   a. sleep
   b. learn
   c. eat
   d. vote

7. If water is **displaced**,
   a. it might freeze
   d. it might boil
   c. it might evaporate
   d. it might spill

8. For **improper** conduct, I would be
   a. scolded
   b. rewarded
   c. praised
   d. ignored

9. Which would you wear when the weather is **brisk**?
   a. a bathing suit
   b. sandals
   c. a sweater
   d. a watch

10. A **considerate** person
    a. is usually late
    b. is a poor loser
    c. is rich and famous
    d. is thoughtful of others

11. Which might be used to **soothe**?
    a. sandpaper
    b. lotion
    c. dynamite
    d. gasoline

12. In the **vicinity** of your face is
    a. your nose
    b. your toe
    c. your knee
    d. your elbow

Definitions

Study the spelling, pronunciation, part of speech, and definition given for each of the words below. Write the word in the blank space in the sentence that follows. Then read the synonyms and antonyms.

1. **abolish** (ə 'bä lish)

   (v.) to do away completely with something; put an end to
   Will human beings ever be able to _____**abolish**_____ *war?*
   SYNONYMS: to outlaw, ban, repeal, stamp out
   ANTONYMS: to establish, restore

2. **appeal** (ə 'pēl)

   (n.) a sincere or strong request for something that is needed; a quality or ability that attracts or interests people; a request to a higher court for review of a legal decision
   Some people don't understand the _____**appeal**_____ *of video games.*
   (v.) to ask strongly for help, understanding, or something else needed; to be attractive or interesting; to request review of a legal decision
   Our class will _____**appeal**_____ *for aid for the homeless.*
   SYNONYMS: a plea, petition; charm, attraction; to plead, implore, beg; to attract
   ANTONYMS: to repel, disgust, repulse

3. **brittle** ('bri təl)

   (adj.) easily broken, snapped, or cracked; not flexible
   The pages of the old book had turned _____**brittle**_____ .
   SYNONYMS: breakable, stiff, unbending, fragile
   ANTONYMS: bendable, flexible, elastic, rugged

4. **condemn** (kən 'dem)

   (v.) to criticize a person or action as wrong, guilty, or evil; to judge as guilty and to punish
   The judge is expected to _____**condemn**_____ *the accused to life imprisonment.*
   SYNONYMS: to disapprove, denounce, blame
   ANTONYMS: to praise, admire, honor, applaud, approve

5. **descend** (di 'send)

   (v.) to move to a lower place from a higher one; to come or be handed down from the past
   We watched the climber _____**descend**_____ *the cliff.*
   SYNONYMS: to drop, fall, plunge, climb down; to stem, derive
   ANTONYMS: to rise, climb, scale, ascend

6. **dictator** ('dik tā tər)

   (n.) a ruler or leader who has total power
   Sometimes my older brother acts like a _____**dictator**_____ .
   SYNONYMS: tyrant, master, despot, oppressor

Frederick Douglass was an escaped slave who became a leader in the movement to **abolish** (word 1) slavery. His autobiography has become a classic of American literature.

7. **expand** ✓
   (ik 'spand)

   (v.) to open up, make or grow larger; to develop
   The principal plans to _____ expand _____ our classroom.

   SYNONYMS: to spread, stretch, swell, enlarge
   ANTONYMS: to shrink, reduce, contract, abridge

8. **famine** 8
   ('fa mən)

   (n.) a severe shortage of food over a large area
   Children especially suffered during the _____ famine _____.

   SYNONYMS: hunger, starvation, scarcity, want
   ANTONYMS: feast, plenty

9. **portable** 5
   ('pôr tə bəl)

   (adj.) easily moved or carried
   Dad put a _____ portable _____ crib in the trunk.

   SYNONYMS: movable, transportable
   ANTONYMS: immovable, fixed, rooted

10. **prey** 9
    (prā)

    (n.) an animal hunted as food by another; someone or something that is helpless against attack
    The documentary showed a lion stalking its _____ prey _____.

    (v.) (used with *on* or *upon*) to hunt for food; to harm, rob, or take advantage of
    Only a bully would _____ prey _____ upon the weak.

    SYNONYMS: a victim; quarry; to devour; to bully, victimize, cheat
    ANTONYMS: a hunter, predator

11. **thrifty** 6
    ('thrif tē)

    (adj.) careful about spending money; tending to save money; managing money well
    My parents are teaching me to be a _____ thrifty _____ shopper.

    SYNONYMS: economical, frugal, tight-fisted
    ANTONYMS: wasteful, careless, extravagant

12. **visual** 1
    ('vi zhə wəl)

    (adj.) having to do with sight or seeing
    The math teacher likes to use _____ visual _____ aids.

    SYNONYMS: visible, pictured, shown, illustrated

Match the Meaning

For each item choose the word whose meaning is suggested by the clue given. Then write the word in the space provided.

1. To judge an action as wrong is to _____ **condemn** _____ it.
   a. condemn   b. descend   c. expand   d. abolish

2. New rooms will _____ **expand** _____ the museum's exhibit space.
   a. condemn   b. expand   c. abolish   d. descend

3. Something that is hunted is called _____ **prey** _____.
   a. dictator   b. famine   c. appeal   d. prey

4. An object that you can pick up and carry with you could be described as _____ **portable** _____.
   a. brittle   b. visual   c. portable   d. thrifty

5. A serious food shortage might cause a(n) _____ **famine** _____.
   a. prey   b. appeal   c. dictator   d. famine

6. To put an end to something is to _____ **abolish** _____ it.
   a. appeal   b. abolish   c. descend   d. expand

7. Something that attracts is said to have _____ **appeal** _____.
   a. appeal   b. famine   c. dictator   d. prey

8. A ruler who does not share power is a(n) _____ **dictator** _____.
   a. appeal   b. prey   c. dictator   d. famine

9. An object that snaps easily is said to be _____ **brittle** _____.
   a. visual   b. brittle   c. portable   d. thrifty

10. A _____ **visual** _____ experience is one that has to do with sight or seeing.
    a. brittle   b. portable   c. thrifty   d. visual

11. To move downward is to _____ **descend** _____.
    a. expand   b. descend   c. abolish   d. condemn

12. A person who looks for bargains is _____ **thrifty** _____.
    a. thrifty   b. portable   c. visual   d. brittle

Synonyms

For each item below choose the word that is most nearly the **same** in meaning as the word or phrase in **boldface.** Then write your choice on the line provided.

1. a **movable** television
   a. brittle   b. portable   c. thrifty   d. visual   _____portable_____

2. reported on the terrible **scarcity**
   a. appeal   b. prey   c. dictator   d. famine   _____famine_____

3. a powerful and selfish **tyrant**
   a. prey   b. famine   c. appeal   d. dictator   _____dictator_____

4. **plead** for help
   a. abolish   b. descend   c. appeal   d. prey   _____appeal_____

5. **pictured** proof of the break-in
   a. visual   b. brittle   c. thrifty   d. portable   _____visual_____

6. turned easily **breakable** by the cold
   a. brittle   b. visual   c. portable   d. thrifty   _____brittle_____

Antonyms

For each item below choose the word that is most nearly **opposite** in meaning to the word or phrase in **boldface.** Then write your choice on the line provided.

1. **shrink** the size of the project
   a. expand   b. descend   c. appeal   d. condemn   _____expand_____

2. tracked the **predator**
   a. dictator   b. prey   c. appeal   d. famine   _____prey_____

3. **restore** the tax on medicine
   a. condemn   b. descend   c. abolish   d. expand   _____abolish_____

4. **praised** the decision
   a. appealed   b. descended   c. abolished   d. condemned   _____condemned_____

5. a **wasteful** consumer
   a. portable   b. visual   c. thrifty   d. brittle   _____thrifty_____

6. **ascend** the mountain
   a. prey upon   b. descend   c. abolish   d. expand   _____descend_____

Unit 10 ■ *85*

Completing the Sentence

From the list of words on pages 82–83, choose the one that best completes each item below. Write the word in the space provided. (You may have to change the word's ending.)

AN END TO SLAVERY

■ Before the Civil War, many northerners _____condemned_____ slavery as a terrible evil, but few wanted to go war because of it. Abraham Lincoln, too, personally hated slavery, but was prepared to accept it if by doing so the Union could be preserved.

■ Once the war began, however, many in the north argued that the time had come to _____abolish_____ slavery once and for all. In 1863 Lincoln issued the Emancipation Proclamation, freeing slaves in the states of the Confederacy.

■ Abraham Lincoln's enemies called him a(n) _____dictator_____ because he exercised so much power during the war.

■ Illustrators and photographers accompanied Union troops during some of the War's bloodiest campaigns, leaving us an important _____visual_____ record of the horrors experienced by the soldiers of both sides of the conflict.

■ Some African Americans who have _____descended_____ from slave families have passed along dramatic stories of their ancestors' experiences.

DROUGHT LEADS TO HUNGER

■ Without enough water, plant fibers dry out and become _____brittle_____. If a drought lasts for a long time, plants and crops die.

■ If too many plants die, insects have no food, and the birds and animals that _____prey_____ on insects then lose their food supply, too.

■ The threat of _____famine_____ often drives animals great distances in search of food.

■ If these animals do not _____expand_____ their hunting area, they too will starve.

A TEACHER ON A BUDGET

■ It would help our teacher a lot to have a _____portable_____ computer that she could take back and forth between school and her home.

■ She has asked businesses to donate any equipment that they no longer need. So far, more than a dozen businesses have answered her _____appeal_____ with computers and monitors for our classroom.

■ It has been a very _____thrifty_____ way of modernizing our classroom because it has cost hardly anything at all.

*Circle the letter next to the word or expression that best completes the sentence or answers the question. Pay special attention to the word in **boldface**.*

1. A **dictator** is most likely
   a. to be loved
   b. to be honored
   c. to be elected
   d. to be feared

2. If a book **appeal**s to you,
   a. you will probably read it
   b. it is probably very long
   c. it is probably boring
   d. you will never read it

3. Which would most likely be **condemned**?
   a. promptness
   b. cruelty
   c. generosity
   d. kindness

4. A **thrifty** person would
   a. give all of her money away
   b. never buy anything on sale
   c. count every penny
   d. leave a generous tip

5. If a rule is **abolished**,
   a. it must be obeyed
   b. it is in effect only one day
   c. it is no longer in effect
   d. it lasts forever

6. Which is a **visual** aid?
   a. a cane
   b. a set of false teeth
   c. a crutch
   d. a pair of glasses

7. If a **famine** struck,
   a. water would be scarce
   b. food would be scarce
   c. money would be scarce
   d. gasoline would be scarce

8. Which is a bird of **prey**?
   a. a canary
   a. a robin
   a. a hummingbird
   d. a hawk

9. Which might you **descend**?
   a. a ladder
   b. a lake
   c. a lily
   d. a lasso

10. If my waistline **expands**, I get
    a. taller
    b. bigger around the middle
    c. shorter
    d. smaller around the middle

11. If something is **brittle**,
    a. it breaks easily
    b. it freezes quickly
    c. it is hard to see
    d. it is easy to carry

12. Which type of house is meant to be **portable**?
    a. a 15-room mansion
    b. a house trailer
    c. a log cabin
    d. a school house

Definitions

Study the spelling, pronunciation, part of speech, and definition given for each of the words below. Write the word in the blank space in the sentence that follows. Then read the synonyms and antonyms.

1. **absurd**
   (əb ′sərd)

   (adj.) making no sense at all, going completely against or having no reason

   No one is going to believe such an _____absurd_____ story!

   SYNONYMS: silly, ridiculous, foolish, crazy, insane
   ANTONYMS: sensible, wise, intelligent, sound

2. **avalanche**
   (′a və lanch)

   (n.) a large mass of snow, ice, rocks, or other material sliding or falling swiftly down a mountainside; something resembling such an event

   The skiers were almost buried by an _____avalanche_____ that came roaring down the slope.

   SYNONYMS: a landslide, flood, cascade

3. **classify**
   (′kla sə fī)

   (v.) to group or label in an organized way

   Libraries usually _____classify_____ books by title, author, and subject.

   SYNONYMS: to order, arrange, sort, catalog, pigeonhole

4. **ensure**
   (in ′shůr)

   (v.) to make sure, safe, or certain; to guarantee

   The playground was designed to _____ensure_____ the children's safety.

   SYNONYMS: to confirm, insure, guarantee
   ANTONYMS: to risk, endanger

5. **navigate**
   (′na və gāt)

   (v.) to plan and steer the course of a vessel or vehicle; to make one's way, get around

   A pilot came aboard to _____navigate_____ the steamboat down the river.

   SYNONYMS: to guide, pilot, operate

6. **nestle**
   (′ne səl)

   (v.) to settle down comfortably; to hold lovingly

   When I was little, I liked to _____nestle_____ in my grandmother's lap.

   SYNONYMS: to cuddle, snuggle

A pilot uses charts and instruments to **navigate** (word 5) a heliocopter.

7. **plea**
   (plē)

   (n.) an urgent request for help; the answer given in a law court by a person accused of a crime

   The defendant entered a _____plea_____ *of not guilty.*

   SYNONYMS: an appeal, cry, petition, prayer

8. **principle**
   ('prin sə pəl)

   (n.) a basic rule or law on which others are based; a belief used to tell right from wrong

   A judge must be a person of high _____principles_____ .

   SYNONYMS: a standard, truth, guide, guideline, creed

9. **realistic**
   (rē ə 'lis tik)

   (adj.) using facts and good sense to evaluate people, things, or situations; concerned with the practical; resembling real life

   The painting was so _____realistic_____ *that it looked like a photograph.*

   SYNONYMS: achievable, reasonable, sensible; true-to-life
   ANTONYMS: impractical, dreamy, unrealistic, pie-in-the-sky

10. **security**
    (si 'kyur ə tē)

    (n.) freedom from danger, fear, or doubt; safety

    There is always heavy _____security_____ *around the White House.*

    SYNONYMS: protection, safekeeping, confidence, assurance
    ANTONYMS: doubt, insecurity, danger, peril

11. **selective**
    (sə 'lek tiv)

    (adj.) very careful about choosing or using

    It pays to be a very _____selective_____ *shopper.*

    SYNONYMS: choosy, particular, picky, fussy, discriminating
    ANTONYMS: unselective, careless

12. **tart**
    (tärt)

    (adj.) having a sharp or sour taste; sharp in manner or tone

    My sister replied with a very _____tart_____ *remark.*

    (n.) a small pie, usually filled with fruit

    I had a peach _____tart_____ *for dessert.*

    SYNONYMS: tangy, acid; biting, cutting, harsh; a pastry
    ANTONYMS: sweet; mild, gentle

Match the Meaning

For each item choose the word whose meaning is suggested by the clue given. Then write the word in the space provided.

1. To cuddle up with something is to _____ **nestle** _____.
   a. nestle   b. navigate   c. ensure   d. classify

2. If you make sure of something, you _____ **ensure** _____ it.
   a. nestle   b. ensure   c. classify   d. navigate

3. A person of high _____ **principles** _____ will always try to do good.
   a. avalanches   b. securities   c. pleas   d. principles

4. A fussy cat will be _____ **selective** _____ about what it eats.
   a. absurd   b. realistic   c. selective   d. tart

5. Freedom from fear leads to a sense of _____ **security** _____.
   a. principle   b. plea   c. avalanche   d. security

6. To decide how to label an item is to _____ **classify** _____ it.
   a. ensure   b. classify   c. navigate   d. nestle

7. An urgent appeal is a(n) _____ **plea** _____ for help.
   a. plea   b. security   c. avalanche   d. principle

8. Snow tumbling down a mountain is called a(n) _____ **avalanche** _____.
   a. plea   b. principle   c. avalanche   d. security

9. A statement that makes no sense is _____ **absurd** _____.
   a. realistic   b. absurd   c. selective   d. tart

10. If you judge a school on facts and evidence, you will probably get a(n) _____ **realistic** _____ sense of the place.
    a. absurd   b. selective   c. tart   d. realistic

11. To steer around obstacles is to _____ **navigate** _____ safely.
    a. ensure   b. navigate   c. classify   d. nestle

12. Lemonade without sugar tastes _____ **tart** _____.
    a. tart   b. selective   c. realistic   d. absurd

Synonyms

For each item below choose the word that is most nearly the **same** in meaning as the word or phrase in **boldface.** Then write your choice on the line provided.

1. questioned our **standards**
   a. principles   b. securities   c. pleas   d. avalanches   _principles_

2. a **landslide** of mail at holiday time
   a. plea   b. security   c. principle   d. avalanche   _avalanche_

3. **appeal** to save the rain forest
   a. classify   b. navigate   c. plea   d. ensure   _plea_

4. **sort** the blocks by shape and color
   a. navigate   b. ensure   c. nestle   d. classify   _classify_

5. **cuddle** in my mother's arms
   a. classify   b. nestle   c. ensure   d. navigate   _nestle_

6. **pilot** a tanker through the canal
   a. ensure   b. navigate   c. classify   d. nestle   _navigate_

Antonyms

For each item below choose the word that is most nearly **opposite** in meaning to the word or phrase in **boldface.** Then write your choice on the line provided.

1. to **deny** safe passage
   a. ensure   b. classify   c. navigate   d. nestle   _ensure_

2. a **sound** excuse for being absent
   a. tart   b. absurd   c. realistic   d. selective   _absurd_

3. show very **careless** taste
   a. selective   b. realistic   c. absurd   d. tart   _selective_

4. an **impractical** view of the situation
   a. absurd   b. realistic   c. selective   d. tart   _realistic_

5. prefer **sweet** apples
   a. selective   b. realistic   c. tart   d. absurd   _tart_

6. felt a sense of **danger**
   a. avalanche   b. security   c. plea   d. principle   _security_

Completing the Sentence

From the list of words on pages 88–89, choose the one that best completes each item below. Then write the word in the space provided. (You may have to change the word's ending.)

A DOG'S LIFE

■ Some dogs are grouped by breed or by the work that they do. Collies and komondors, for example, are labeled as herding dogs because they are both used to protect and herd sheep. Highly trained dogs that work to help people are _____classified_____ as assistance dogs.

■ Handlers of these animals have to be very _____selective_____ in choosing dogs for the demanding training. Some animals are simply not suited to the work.

■ Some dogs, like police or guard dogs, offer _____security_____ from crime or trespassers, helping their owners feel safer in their homes. German shepherds and Doberman pinschers are among the best known of these breeds.

■ Rescue dogs can go where humans can not or dare not go. For example, these dogs can safely _____navigate_____ the ruins or rubble left by earthquakes or accidents, in search of survivors.

■ Large, strong dogs with thick fur, such as St. Bernards or huskies, are trained to rescue skiers or climbers trapped by _____avalanches_____.

■ Schools for these remarkable dogs make yearly _____pleas_____ for money and for volunteers who will help prepare puppies for "canine careers."

CLOWNING AROUND

■ Like other schools, the Ringling Brothers Clown College is guided by a philosophy of education. At the Clown College, the first and foremost _____principle_____ is that just about anyone can be taught the art of clowning.

■ To _____ensure_____ success as clowns, students must work hard to master many skills, including juggling, acrobatics, make-up design, and comedy writing.

■ Great clowns make sensible, ordinary tasks, like opening a box, somehow seem _____absurd_____ and wacky.

■ Sarcastic clowns use insults and _____tart_____ comments to get laughs. Occasionally they make fun of people in the audience, but usually the clowns themselves are the butts of their own jokes.

■ In one funny routine, a clown dressed as a porcupine _____nestled_____ against a cactus and called it "Mama."

■ The cactus looked quite _____realistic_____ and life-like from a distance, but on closer inspection it proved to be made of rubber.

Circle the letter next to the word or expression that best completes the sentence or answers the question. Pay special attention to the word in **boldface.**

1. Which would be an **absurd** gift for a two-year-old?
   a. a toy drum
   b. a beach ball
   c. a dinosaur puppet
   d. a real sports car

2. Where might you see an **avalanche**?
   a. on the ocean
   b. in the mountains
   c. on a desert
   d. in a suburb

3. You *cannot* be **classified** as
   a. a mammal
   b. a student
   c. a human being
   d. a plant

4. Which is a **plea**?
   a. "Thank you!"
   b. "That's an order!"
   c. "I forgot my lunch."
   d. "Not guilty, your honor."

5. Athletes with strong **principles**
   a. play by the rules
   b. fight with the coach
   c. hold out for more money
   d. skip practice

6. Studying hard will help **ensure**
   a. good manners
   b. good looks
   c. good weather
   d. good grades

7. Which will probably be **tart**?
   a. honey
   b. butterscotch pudding
   c. lemon juice
   d. blueberry pie

8. If a kitten **nestles**
   a. it scratches and howls
   b. it cuddles and purrs
   c. it chases a mouse
   d. it laps up milk

9. A movie about a **realistic** situation might be titled
   a. "I Married an Alligator!"
   b. "The Magic Eggplant"
   c. "Forest Fire!"
   d. "Martian Dance Party"

10. A sense of **security** makes you feel
    a. upset
    b. nervous
    c. safe
    d. lucky

11. A **selective** person might be called
    a. "Pokey Polly"
    b. "Picky Peter"
    c. "Wacky William"
    d. "Forgetful Fran"

12. Which is easiest to **navigate**?
    a. a bicycle
    b. a hot air balloon
    c. a bucking bronco
    d. a sailboat

UNIT 12

Definitions

Study the spelling, pronunciation, part of speech, and definition given for each of the words below. Write the word in the blank space in the sentence that follows. Then read the synonyms and antonyms.

1. **abuse**
   (*n.*, ə 'byüs;
   v., ə 'byüz)

   (n.) improper, wrong, or cruel treatment; insulting language
   The _____abuse_____ of power is a danger in any government.

   (v.) to put to bad use; to hurt or damage by treating badly
   If you _____abuse_____ your privileges, they may be taken away.

   SYNONYMS: misuse, mistreatment; to harm, injure; to insult
   ANTONYMS: care, support; to cherish, honor, praise

2. **appliance**
   (ə 'plī əns)

   (n.) a machine or tool used to do a household job
   It seemed an awfully big claim for such a little _____appliance_____.

   SYNONYMS: a tool, device, utensil, contraption, gadget

3. **confirm**
   (kən 'fərm)

   (v.) to agree or prove that something is true; to make sure, remove any doubt
   The press secretary refused to _____confirm_____ the report.

   SYNONYMS: to verify, agree, support, assure; to check
   ANTONYMS: to deny, disprove; to cancel

4. **daze**
   (dāz)

   (v.) to stun or confuse
   Some predators _____daze_____ their prey with a blow to the head.

   (n.) a state of confusion
   When I heard that I had won the prize, I walked around in a _____daze_____.

   SYNONYMS: to numb, shock, astound, baffle, bewilder; a trance, stupor

5. **flimsy**
   ('flim zē)

   (adj.) not strong or solid; poorly made; not convincing
   I don't think my teacher believed my _____flimsy_____ excuse for not doing my homework.

   SYNONYMS: thin, light, weak, rickety, feeble; shabby, shoddy
   ANTONYMS: strong, sturdy, sound; convincing

6. **gauge**
   (gāj)

   (n.) a standard measure used to tell size, thickness, and so on; an instrument used to measure
   Weather scientists use a _____gauge_____ to measure rainfall.

   (v.) to measure; to estimate
   The cat seemed to _____gauge_____ the distance before jumping onto the windowsill.

   SYNONYMS: a scale, rule, yardstick; to judge, assess; to guess

94

Ballerinas are taught to **rotate** (word 11)
while balancing on one toe in order
to perform pirouettes, or spins.

7. **migrant**
('mī grənt)

(n.) an animal or person that moves from one region to another as
the seasons change; a farm worker who moves seasonally to pick
different crops

We passed a field full of _____migrants_____ picking berries.

SYNONYMS: a traveler, nomad, drifter

8. **neutral**
('nü trəl)

(adj.) not taking any side in a disagreement or war; in-between,
lacking distinction; not in gear

*Switzerland remained _____neutral_____ through both World
Wars I and II.*

SYNONYMS: uninvolved, uncommitted, impartial, open-minded; indefinite, vague
ANTONYMS: involved, committed, opinionated, heated; bold

9. **pitiless**
('pi ti ləs)

(adj.) showing no sorrow or regret for another's suffering or troubles

The audience booed the _____pitiless_____ villain.

SYNONYMS: cold, merciless, heartless, unsparing, cruel
ANTONYMS: kindhearted, merciful, sympathetic

10. **presentable**
(pri 'zen tə bəl)

(adj.) fit to be seen or inspected

My parents insisted that I wear _____presentable_____ clothing.

SYNONYMS: suitable, proper, respectable, passable
ANTONYMS: shabby, improper, unfit, unacceptable

11. **rotate**
('rō tāt)

(v.) to turn around a central point; to alternate

Do you know how long it takes Earth to _____rotate_____ once?

SYNONYMS: to circle, twirl, spin; to change, switch

12. **shred**
(shred)

(n.) a thin strip; a tiny piece or amount

Not a _____shred_____ of evidence was found.

(v.) to cut or tear into thin strips or small pieces; to rip up

The secretary was asked to _____shred_____ the document.

SYNONYMS: a scrap, tatter, bit, fragment
ANTONYMS: a whole; to fix, mend, repair

Match the Meaning

For each item choose the word whose meaning is suggested by the clue given. Then write the word in the space provided.

1. To use something in a way that brings harm to yourself or others is to _____**abuse**_____ it.
   a. gauge   b. rotate   c. daze   d. abuse

2. If you have been stunned, you might be in a(n) _____**daze**_____ .
   a. gauge   b. daze   c. appliance   d. shred

3. To tear something to pieces is to _____**shred**_____ it.
   a. abuse   b. daze   c. shred   d. rotate

4. A _____**pitiless**_____ foe would not show mercy.
   a. flimsy   b. presentable   c. pitiless   d. neutral

5. Not to take sides is to remain _____**neutral**_____ .
   a. pitiless   b. presentable   c. flimsy   d. neutral

6. To prove something is to _____**confirm**_____ it.
   a. daze   b. confirm   c. rotate   d. gauge

7. People or animals that move to different regions as the seasons change are called _____**migrants**_____ .
   a. migrants   b. gauges   c. appliances   d. shreds

8. Blenders and can openers are kitchen _____**appliances**_____ .
   a. migrants   b. shreds   c. appliances   d. gauges

9. Something poorly made is said to be _____**flimsy**_____ .
   a. presentable   b. flimsy   c. pitiless   d. neutral

10. A room fit to be inspected is _____**presentable**_____ .
    a. flimsy   b. pitiless   c. neutral   d. presentable

11. To alternate chores is to _____**rotate**_____ them.
    a. shred   b. rotate   c. abuse   d. gauge

12. You would use a _____**gauge**_____ to measure something.
    a. gauge   b. shred   c. daze   d. migrant

Synonyms

*For each item below choose the word that is most nearly the **same** in meaning as the word or phrase in **boldface**. Then write your choice on the line provided.*

1. an electrical **device** for cleaning rugs
   a. shred   b. migrant   c. gauge   d. appliance   _____appliance_____

2. left behind by the **drifters**
   a. shreds   b. abuses   c. migrants   d. gauges   _____migrants_____

3. wore a **respectable** outfit for the class picture
   a. presentable   b. flimsy   c. neutral   d. pitiless   _____presentable_____

4. **numbed** by the terrible news
   a. gauged   b. dazed   c. rotated   d. confirmed   _____dazed_____

5. **assess** the value of the coin collection
   a. shred   b. gauge   c. abuse   d. rotate   _____gauge_____

6. **twirl** the plant to face the sun
   a. confirm   b. gauge   c. daze   d. rotate   _____rotate_____

Antonyms

*For each item below choose the word that is most nearly **opposite** in meaning to the word or phrase in **boldface**. Then write your choice on the line provided.*

1. **mend** the old pillowcase
   a. shred   b. confirm   c. rotate   d. gauge   _____shred_____

2. **sturdy** shoes
   a. abused   b. flimsy   c. presentable   d. pitiless   _____flimsy_____

3. reported their **kindhearted** treatment
   a. neutral   b. flimsy   c. presentable   d. pitiless   _____pitiless_____

4. refused to **deny** the rumor
   a. gauge   b. rotate   c. confirm   d. classify   _____confirm_____

5. painted in **bold** colors
   a. flimsy   b. neutral   c. realistic   d. pitiless   _____neutral_____

6. fans who **praise** the umpires
   a. rotate   b. classify   c. abuse   d. daze   _____abuse_____

Completing the Sentence

From the list of words on pages 94–95, choose the one that best completes each item below. Then write the word in the space provided. (You may have to change the word's ending.)

A TOAST TO TOAST

■ One of the most common of household _____**appliances**_____, the electric toaster, was first introduced to American kitchens in 1910.

■ Early models toasted only one side of the bread at a time. In order to toast both sides, you had to _____**rotate**_____ the slice of bread yourself.

■ These toasters did not have self-timers, either. If you didn't pay careful attention, your toast might not look very _____**presentable**_____. And if it had turned to ashes, it might not even be fit to eat!

FROM FIELD TO FIELD

■ It is estimated that in the United States there are today about half a million _____**migrants**_____ who follow the harvest each year in search of work at fruit and vegetable farms.

■ Unfortunately, these workers are often _____**abused**_____ by harsh bosses who pay too little and demand too much. To make matters worse, working and living conditions are often unsafe and unsanitary.

■ Bending over for hours under a hot sun to harvest crops can leave these workers feeling _____**dazed**_____ by the end of a long day in the fields.

■ The _____**pitiless**_____ sun beats down on the workers, offering no mercy to man, woman, or child.

■ Some farm workers are so poor that they barely get enough to eat, and their old, tattered clothes hang in _____**shreds**_____.

■ Rather than stay _____**neutral**_____ about the problems that seasonal farm workers face, some activists are taking up their cause by fighting for improved legal and civil rights.

RUNNING ON EMPTY

■ When our car came sputtering to a stop on a dark and lonely country road, I was almost afraid to look at the fuel _____**gauge**_____.

■ But when I did, a quick glance was enough to _____**confirm**_____ the worst: the car had run out of gas, just as I suspected.

■ We had to walk two miles to a gas station, with nothing more to protect us from the rain than our _____**flimsy**_____ jackets. When we got back to the car with a container of fuel, we were completely soaked and shivering with cold.

*Circle the letter next to the word or expression that best completes the sentence or answers the question. Pay special attention to the word in **boldface**.*

1. A **flimsy** toy will probably
   a. cost lots of money
   b. break much too soon
   c. be very popular
   d. come in many colors

2. To **confirm** a fact for a social studies report, you might
   a. check an encyclopedia
   b. read a science-fiction novel
   c. copy the paper neatly
   d. call your doctor

3. If you're in a **daze**, you may
   a. yell at your friends
   b. remember to water the plants
   c. not notice the time
   d. turn the calendar page

4. Birds that are **migrants** probably
   a. have blue feathers
   b. lay only one egg at a time
   c. eat fruits and vegetables
   d. travel in the spring and fall

5. Which is known for **rotating**?
   a. a teddy bear
   b. a top
   c. a book
   d. a sandwich

6. A **neutral** nation would not be
   a. in debt
   b. an island
   c. at war
   d. at peace

7. Which is easiest to **shred**?
   a. a loaf of bread
   b. a brass ring
   c. a suit of armor
   d. a spike

8. A piano that has been **abused**
   a. would sound better
   b. might be out of tune
   c. would increase in value
   d. might be hard to move

9. A **pitiless** person would make others
   a. feel unloved
   b. feel unfamiliar
   c. feel at ease
   d. feel proud

10. Which might you need to **gauge**?
    a. the distance from Earth to the moon
    b. a friend's height
    c. the amount of gold in Fort Knox
    d. the width of a cat's whisker

11. To make your room more **presentable**, you might
    a. feed your hamster
    b. put away your clothes and toys
    c. open the window
    d. lock the door

12. Which is an **appliance**?
    a. a box of laundry detergent
    b. a laundry room
    c. a laundry basket
    d. a washing machine

Selecting Word Meanings

*For each of the following items circle the choice that is most nearly the **same** in meaning as the word in **boldface.***

1. check the latest opinion **poll**
   a. speech   (b.) survey   c. software   d. timetable

2. learn **thrifty** habits
   (a.) money-saving   b. childish   c. wasteful   d. nervous

3. **rotate** the schedule
   a. write   b. memorize   (c.) switch   d. stick to

4. **identical** patterns
   (a.) matching   b. complicated   c. unusual   d. colorful

5. **neutral** reporting
   a. opinionated   b. careless   c. realistic   (d.) unbiased

6. **classify** the types of insects
   a. read about   b. preserve   (c.) catalog   d. photograph

7. **humiliated** the defending champions
   a. congratulated   (b.) embarrassed   c. cheered for   d. disliked

8. **confirm** the dental appointment
   (a.) make sure of   b. reschedule   c. cancel   d. fear

9. studied the **principles** of multiplication
   a. questions   b. challenges   (c.) rules   d. theories

10. a **brisk** early morning swim
    a. slow   b. relaxing   c. exhausting   (d.) energetic

11. **expand** the search
    a. join   (b.) widen   c. end   d. begin

12. **considerate** neighbors
    a. friendly   b. noisy   (c.) thoughtful   d. sneaky

Spelling

For each item below study the **boldface** word in which there is a blank. If a letter is missing, fill in the blank to make a correctly spelled word. If the word is already spelled correctly, leave the blank empty.

1. numbers on a **ga__uge**

2. an **avalanch _e_** of bills

3. **so _o_ the** my aching head

4. a desperate **ple__a**

5. a labor-saving **ap _p_ liance**

6. lost in a **da__ze**

7. **condem _n_** the attack

8. **des _c_ end** a staircase

9. **migr _a_ nt** whales

10. an **abs _u_ rd** suggestion

11. a **present _a_ ble** appearance

12. fought against the **dictat _o_ r**

Antonyms

For each of the following items circle the choice that is most nearly the **opposite** in meaning to the word in **boldface** in the introductory phrase.

1. **confirmed** my fears
   a. explained   (b.) disproved   c. ignored   d. supported

2. **brittle** tree branches
   a. stiff   b. slender   (c.) bendable   d. thick

3. **shred** the old photograph
   (a.) mend   b. tear up   c. throw away   d. lose

4. **tart** fruits
   a. tangy   b. ripe   c. frozen   (d.) sweet

5. speak out against **abuse**
   (a.) kindness   b. mistreatment   c. knowledge   d. humor

6. a **portable** stage
   (a.) fixed   b. movable   c. small   d. bare

7. a **flimsy** explanation
   a. lengthy   b. weak   c. complicated   (d.) convincing

8. **improper** way of doing things
   a. wrong   b. awkward   (c.) correct   d. simple

Vocabulary in Context

Words have been left out of the following passage. For each numbered item in the passage, fill in the circle next to the word in the margin that best fills the blank space. Then answer each question below by writing a sentence that contains one of the words you have chosen.

Scientists use different techniques to find out the number of plants or animals in a given area. To __1__ the population of free-tailed bats in Carlsbad Caverns, New Mexico, scientists videotaped the animals flying out of a cave where they roost in large colonies. Then the scientists counted the bats in each frame of the video.

Sometimes scientists can use just their eyes to determine a population. This purely __2__ method works if the plants or animals are large and their number is small. For example, to count the maple trees in a small area in New England, scientists could use their eyes alone. A more complicated technique would be needed to tell the number of small animals, such as field mice, in the __3__.

Scientists study plant and animal populations for many reasons. They might use the number of a certain kind of fish in a lake to get information about water pollution. They might keep track of populations of protected animals to help __4__ their survival. Or they might count the number of animals of an endangered species to demonstrate that the species needs official protection.

1. ○ abolish
   ○ expand
   ○ cherish
   ● estimate

2. ○ neutral
   ○ thrifty
   ○ selective
   ● visual

3. ● vicinity
   ○ poll
   ○ famine
   ○ avalanche

4. ○ classify
   ○ appeal
   ○ condemn
   ● ensure

5. What method can scientists use to find the number of large animals in a small area?

   Scientists can use a purely **visual** method to gauge this kind of population.

6. Could scientists use this method to tell the number of field mice in the same area?

   Scientists would use another technique to tell the number of mice in the **vicinity**.

7. Why might scientists count a population of protected animals?

   Scientists might count a population of protected animals to **ensure** their continued survival.

8. Why did scientists videotape free-tailed bats flying out of a cave in Carlsbad Caverns?

   Scientists videotaped the bats to **estimate** their population.

Analogies

In each of the following circle the letter for the item that best completes the comparison. Then explain the relationship on the lines provided.

1. **cherish** is to **abuse** as
   a. cuddle is to nestle
   b. displace is to move
   c. (soothe is to excite)
   d. end is to abolish

Relationship: "Cherish" and "abuse" are antonyms/opposite in meaning; "soothe" and "excite" are antonyms/opposite in meaning.

2. **flimsy** is to **weak** as
   a. realistic is to absurd
   b. tart is to sweet
   c. (selective is to choosy)
   d. pitiless is to caring

Relationship: "Flimsy" and "weak" are synonyms/mean the same; "selective" and "choosy" are synonyms/mean the same.

3. **brittle** is to **flexible** as
   a. (thrifty is to wasteful)
   b. realistic is to practical
   c. tart is to tangy
   d. pitiless is to cruel

Relationship: The words are antonyms/ have opposite meanings.

4. **famine** is to **food** as
   a. blizzard is to snow
   b. hurricane is to wind
   c. flood is to rain
   d. (drought is to water)

Relationship: A famine occurs when there is a shortage of food; a drought occurs when there is a shortage of water.

Challenge: Make up your own

Write a comparison using the words in the box below. (Hint: There are three possible analogies.) Then write the relationship on the lines provided.

apple	wolf	appeal	gauge
prey	vegetable	measure	fruit
attract	predator	carrot	sheep

Analogy: _____ is to _____ as _____ is to _____.

Relationship: See Table of Contents

Word Families

*The words in **boldface** in the sentences below are related to words introduced in Units 9–12. For example, the nouns* confirmation *and* navigation *in item 1 are related to the verbs* confirm *(Unit 12) and* navigate *(Unit 11). Based on your understanding of the unit words that follow, circle the related word in **boldface** that best completes each sentence.*

poll	portable	rotate	migrant	presentable
humiliate	classify	absurd	confirm	displace
expand	estimate	descend	improper	considerate
navigate	flimsy	neutral	condemn	abuse

1. The U.S. Senate is responsible for the (**confirmation**/**navigation**) of the President's nominees for ambassadorships.

2. Queen Elizabeth II of England is a direct (**classification**/**descendant**) of Queen Victoria.

3. A figure skater who successfully performs a quadruple jump completes four (**rotations**/**considerations**) in the air.

4. A public official who takes a bribe is guilty of (**impropriety**/**absurdity**).

5. Scientists use photographs of the one-of-a-kind markings on the tail fins of humpback whales as one tool in tracking the (**migration**/**expansion**) of these marine mammals.

6. During an election campaign (**pollsters**/**abusers**) question voters about which candidates they prefer.

7. One of the advantages of a personal stereo is its (**presentability**/ **portability**).

8. In math we learn that (**displacement**/**estimation**) can sometimes help us solve problems.

9. While a trial is in progress the judge repeatedly instructs the jury to maintain its (**neutrality**/**flimsiness**) until all the testimony and evidence have been presented.

10. The terrorist attack on innocent civilians received worldwide (**humiliation**/ **condemnation**).

Word Games

Use the clues below to complete the crossword puzzle.
(All of the answers are words from Units 9–13.)

```
 1D                    2V  I  C  I  N  I  T  3Y
 I                                          A
 4S  H  R  E  D                             R
 P                     5R  E  6A  L  I  S  T  I  C
 L                             B
 7F  A  M  I  8N  E     9D  O  W  N  10F A  L  L
 C              E              L      L
 E              S              I      I
       11P  I  T  I  L  E  S  S       M
               L              H      S
       12P  R  E  Y                   Y
```

Down
1. to move aside
3.
6. do away with completely
8. cuddle
10. poorly made

Across
2. neighborhood
4. tear to bits
5. lifelike
7. widespread hunger
9. collapse or ruin
11. without mercy
12. predator's victim

Definitions

Study the spelling, pronunciation, part of speech, and definition given for each of the words below. Write the word in the blank space in the sentence that follows. Then read the synonyms and antonyms.

1. **achievement**
(ə 'chēv mənt)

(n.) something done successfully; something gained by working or trying hard

A perfect report card is quite an _____achievement_____ .

SYNONYMS: an accomplishment, feat, triumph
ANTONYMS: a defeat, failure, setback

2. **acquire**
(ə 'kwīr)

(v.) to get as one's own

When did you _____acquire_____ the ability to speak French so well?

SYNONYMS: to get, obtain, gain, earn
ANTONYMS: to lose, give up, surrender

3. **debate**
(di 'bāt)

(n.) a discussion of reasons for and against something

The town council held a _____debate_____ on building a new library.

(v.) to discuss reasons for and against something; to think about carefully before deciding

What issue would you like to _____debate_____ ?

SYNONYMS: a discussion, argument, dispute; to discuss, consider
ANTONYMS: an agreement; to agree (with)

4. **exhibit**
(ig 'zi bət)

(v.) to show clearly; to put on display

You _____exhibit_____ great talent in gymnastics.

(n.) something shown to the public

We went to the diamond _____exhibit_____ at the science museum.

SYNONYMS: to present, show, reveal; a display, exhibition
ANTONYMS: to hide, conceal, cover up

5. **foe**
(fō)

(n.) one who hates or tries to harm another; an enemy

Identify yourself: Are you friend or _____foe_____ ?

SYNONYMS: an enemy, opponent, rival
ANTONYMS: a friend, ally, comrade, buddy

6. **latter**
('la tər)

(adj.) closer to the end; relating to the second of two things discussed

The first part of the movie is good, but the _____latter_____ part drags on too long.

SYNONYMS: last, later, end, final
ANTONYMS: former, first, earlier, beginning

Some people who make computer parts have to wear special clothing to keep their work area completely **sanitary** (word 10).

7. **massacre**
('ma si kər)

(n.) the cruel killing of many people or animals
The village was the site of a bloody _____massacre_____.

(v.) to kill many people or animals in a cruel way
The barbarians planned to _____massacre_____ their rivals.

SYNONYMS: a slaughter, killing; to butcher, slaughter, kill

8. **monotonous**
(mə 'nä tən əs)

(adj.) dull as a result of not changing in any way
Shelling peas is a _____monotonous_____ chore.

SYNONYMS: boring, uninteresting, tiresome
ANTONYMS: varied, lively, exciting

9. **preserve**
(pri 'zərv)

(v.) to keep safe from injury or ruin; to keep food from spoiling
I signed a petition to _____preserve_____ the wetlands.

(n.) an area set aside for the protection of wildlife
Wild animals roam freely in the nature _____preserve_____.

SYNONYMS: to save, protect, conserve; a refuge, sanctuary
ANTONYMS: to waste, destroy, misuse

10. **sanitary**
('sa nə ter ē)

(adj.) having to do with health; free of dirt and germs
A health inspector checks _____sanitary_____ conditions in a restaurant.

SYNONYMS: clean, pure, sterile, hygienic
ANTONYMS: dirty, filthy, contaminated, unhealthy

11. **sprawl**
(sprôl)

(v.) to lie or sit with arms and legs spread out; to spread out in a disorderly way
Some nights I _____sprawl_____ in front of the TV set.

SYNONYMS: to lounge, slouch, relax, stretch, extend

12. **widespread**
(wīd 'spred)

(adj.) happening in many places or to many people; fully open
Interest in the lives of movie stars is _____widespread_____.

SYNONYMS: far-reaching, vast, common
ANTONYMS: limited, rare, unusual, uncommon

Match the Meaning

For each item below choose the word whose meaning is suggested by the clue given. Then write the word in the space provided.

1. A display of paintings or other objects is a(n) _____exhibit_____.
   a. debate   b. exhibit   c. massacre   d. preserve

2. A belief that is held by many people is _____widespread_____.
   a. latter   b. monotonous   c. widespread   d. sanitary

3. When you buy property, you _____acquire_____ it.
   a. massacre   b. sprawl   c. debate   d. acquire

4. People who hate one another are _____foes_____ .
   a. achievements   b. foes   c. debates   d. exhibits

5. The cruel killing of many innocent people is a(n) _____massacre_____.
   a. massacre   b. exhibit   c. achievement   d. foe

6. Something that is free of germs is _____sanitary_____.
   a. widespread   b. monotonous   c. latter   d. sanitary

7. To consider the pros and cons of an issue is to _____debate_____ it.
   a. debate   b. exhibit   c. preserve   d. acquire

8. A bird sanctuary is an example of a wildlife _____preserve_____.
   a. debate   b. massacre   c. preserve   d. foe

9. The second of two events is the _____latter_____ one.
   a. monotonous   b. latter   c. sanitary   d. widespread

10. Landing on the moon is an example of a(n) _____achievement_____.
    a. foe   b. achievement   c. massacre   d. preserve

11. Something that is done over and over in the same way is _____monotonous_____.
    a. latter   b. widespread   c. sanitary   d. monotonous

12. To lie on the floor with your arms and legs spread out is to _____sprawl_____.
    a. exhibit   b. preserve   c. sprawl   d. acquire

Synonyms

*For each item below choose the word that is most nearly the **same** in meaning as the word or phrase in **boldface**. Then write your choice on the line provided.*

1. a worthy **opponent**
   a. preserve   b. exhibit   c. foe   d. debate   _____foe_____

2. **slaughter** the newborn harp seals
   a. preserve   b. exhibit   c. acquire   d. massacre   _____massacre_____

3. the **boring** refrain of "tra-la-la"
   a. latter   b. sanitary   c. widespread   d. monotonous   ___monotonous___

4. **consider** going by train or by car
   a. sprawl   b. debate   c. acquire   d. massacre   _____debate_____

5. my proudest **accomplishment**
   a. preserve   b. exhibit   c. foe   d. achievement   ___achievement___

6. **lounge** on the couch
   a. exhibit   b. preserve   c. sprawl   d. massacre   _____sprawl_____

Antonyms

*For each item below choose the word that is most nearly **opposite** in meaning to the word or phrase in **boldface**. Then write your choice on the line provided.*

1. **conceal** your surprise
   a. exhibit   b. sprawl   c. massacre   d. preserve   _____exhibit_____

2. the **first** of the two dates
   a. widespread   b. latter   c. monotonous   d. sanitary   _____latter_____

3. **lose** millions of dollars
   a. debate   b. sprawl   c. massacre   d. acquire   _____acquire_____

4. **limited** appeal among children
   a. sanitary   b. monotonous c. latter   d. widespread   ___widespread___

5. **destroy** the town records
   a. massacre   b. exhibit   c. preserve   d. sprawl   _____preserve_____

6. found **unhealthy** living conditions
   a. latter   b. sanitary   c. widespread   d. monotonous   _____sanitary_____

Completing the Sentence

From the list of words on pages 106–107, choose the one that best completes each item below. Write the word in the space provided. (You may have to change the word's ending.)

YOU CAN'T WIN THEM ALL

■ The current events club had to decide whether to _____**debate**_____ hunters' rights or the child helmet law.

■ We chose the child helmet law, the _____**latter**_____ issue, because it was more relevant to students our age.

■ The members of our team gave such _____**monotonous**_____ speeches in favor of the law that the other team won, although their arguments were more emotional than fact-filled.

WHAT HAPPENED IN RWANDA

■ In 1994 a brutal _____**massacre**_____ took place in Rwanda, a country in Central Africa. Hundreds of thousands of people on both sides were injured or killed.

■ The major _____**foes**_____ were the Hutu and Tutsi peoples, whose tribes have been in conflict for generations.

■ In overcrowded refugee camps, _____**sanitary**_____ conditions were dangerously poor. Clean water, food, and medicines were in short supply.

■ Rescue workers found entire families _____**sprawled**_____ on the ground. Many of these people were dying of starvation and disease.

"FOUR SCORE AND SEVEN YEARS AGO. . ."

■ Many historians consider Abraham Lincoln's Gettysburg Address to be the greatest _____**achievement**_____ in public speaking this nation has produced.

■ The fame of this brief speech is so _____**widespread**_____ that most Americans—and even many from other nations—know the opening of it by heart.

■ The Library of Congress _____**acquired**_____ a copy of the speech, written in Lincoln's own hand. Only four other copies in his handwriting are still in existence.

■ At the library the manuscript is carefully _____**preserved**_____ as a national historical treasure.

■ Sometimes the document travels to Pennsylvania for _____**exhibit**_____ in connection with special events at the actual site of the battle. The battlefield became a national park in 1895.

Word Associations

*Circle the letter next to the word or expression that best completes the sentence or answers the question. Pay special attention to the word in **boldface**.*

1. A cafeteria that is **sanitary** has
   a. good main dishes
   b. overflowing trash bins
   c. safely prepared food
   d. high-priced lunches

2. The **latter** part of December includes
   a. the first day of the month
   b. the last week of the month
   c. four Sundays
   d. New Year's Day

3. If my neighbor is my **foe,** we
   a. share a driveway
   b. do not get along
   c. live in the country
   d. feed each other's pets

4. Witnesses to a **massacre** probably feel
   a. horrified
   b. cheerful
   c. hungry
   d. relaxed

5. A **monotonous** speaker might
   a. win an award for public speaking
   b. wake up the neighborhood
   c. give speech lessons
   d. put a listener to sleep

6. A swimmer who is honored for his or her **achievements** might
   a. go waterskiing
   b. get a sunburn
   c. get a trophy
   d. go to an aquarium

7. Which of these has been **preserved**?
   a. apples on a tree
   b. berries on a vine
   c. fresh peach pie
   d. canned pears

8. Which might be included in an **exhibit** of students' work?
   a. paintings by famous artists
   b. science fair projects
   c. parents and teachers
   d. rulers and erasers

9. One way to **acquire** a rare stamp is to
   a. mail a letter
   b. read a book about collecting stamps
   c. buy one from a catalog
   d. pay extra postage

10. A participant in a **debate** should
   a. defend his or her point of view
   b. try not to say anything
   c. never argue with an opponent
   d. join the football team

11. Which of these is **widespread**?
   a. an opinion held by a few friends
   b. a belief that the earth is flat
   c. an interest in fruitflies
   d. a disease that infects many people

12. I might **sprawl** on the couch to
   a. relax
   b. wake up
   c. move furniture
   d. exercise

Definitions

Study the spelling, pronunciation, part of speech, and definition given for each of the words below. Write the word in the blank space in the sentence that follows. Then read the synonyms and antonyms.

1. **alibi**
('a lə bī)

(n.) a claim of having been elsewhere when a crime was committed; a reason given to explain something
Can anyone confirm your _____alibi_____?
SYNONYMS: an excuse, explanation, story, defense

2. **confederate**
(kən 'fe də rət)

(adj.) joined with others for a common purpose
Seven sheikdoms are _____confederate_____ states in the United Arab Emirates.

(n.) a person, state, or country that joins with another for a common purpose; a partner in crime
Some of our wartime allies are still our _____confederates_____ in peace keeping organizations.
SYNONYMS: united, allied, combined; an ally, accomplice
ANTONYMS: divided, separated; a foe, enemy

3. **discharge**
(v., dis 'chärj;
n., 'dis chärj)

(v.) to let go; to unload cargo or passengers; to fire off; to give off
Did the hospital _____discharge_____ the patient?

(n.) a release or letting go; a firing off; a giving off; something given off
A search of the records showed that the army gave the soldier an honorable _____discharge_____.
SYNONYMS: to release, dismiss, shoot; a dismissal, release
ANTONYMS: to detain, imprison; to hire, appoint; to load, absorb

4. **economical**
(e kə 'nä mi kəl)

(adj.) careful about spending money or using resources
An _____economical_____ shopper waits for sales and always looks for a bargain.
SYNONYMS: thrifty, frugal, saving
ANTONYMS: extravagant, wasteful

5. **frank**
(fraŋk)

(adj.) honest in expressing thoughts and feelings
Don't be offended if I am _____frank_____ with you.
SYNONYMS: direct, blunt, straightforward, truthful
ANTONYMS: secretive, insincere, dishonest

6. **modify**
('mä də fī)

(v.) to change somewhat
A good cook knows how to _____modify_____ a recipe if one or two of the ingredients are not available.
SYNONYMS: to adjust, alter, adapt, vary, revise

7. **mutiny**
('myü tən ē)

(n.) an open rebellion against authority
The Boston Tea Party was an act of _____ mutiny _____.

(v.) to rebel against those in charge
The captain's cruelty led the crew to _____ mutiny _____.

SYNONYMS: a revolt, uprising, riot; to revolt, rise up
ANTONYMS: to support, obey

8. **negative**
('ne gə tiv)

(adj.) saying "no"; not positive or helpful; less than zero; having the same electric charge as an electron
The reply to my question was _____ negative _____.

(n.) an expression that says "no"; a photographic image in which light and dark areas are reversed
"I can't" is an example of a _____ negative _____.

SYNONYMS: bad, unfavorable
ANTONYMS: positive, helpful, good, favorable

9. **pursue**
(pər 'sü)

(v.) to chase in order to catch; to strive to achieve; to carry out
During a hunt the dogs _____ pursue _____ *a hare.*

SYNONYMS: to follow, hunt, run after, aim for, work for
ANTONYMS: to run away, take off, flee, bolt

10. **reign**
(rān)

(n.) the power or rule of a monarch; a monarch's period of rule
England prospered under the _____ reign _____ *of Queen Anne.*

(v.) to rule as a monarch; to be widespread
During the 1920s, prosperity _____ reigned _____.

SYNONYMS: the regime, rule, control; to govern, command

11. **singular**
('siŋ gyə lər)

(adj.) referring to one person or thing only; out of the ordinary
"Is" is a _____ singular _____ *verb.*

(n.) the form of a word that is used to refer to one person or thing
"Mouse" is the _____ singular _____ *of "mice."*

SYNONYMS: exceptional, unusual
ANTONYMS: plural; a plural

12. **swindle**
('swin dəl)

(v.) to cheat out of money or property
A dishonest shopkeeper tried to _____ swindle _____ *me.*

(n.) a scheme for cheating someone
The fraud squad uncovered the _____ swindle _____.

SYNONYMS: to deceive, trick, gyp, con; a scam, fraud, hoax, racket

113

Match the Meaning

For each item below choose the word whose meaning is suggested by the clue given. Then write the word in the space provided.

1. To rebel against commanding officers is to _____**mutiny**_____ .
   a. discharge   b. swindle   c. modify   d. mutiny

2. To exercise the powers of a king or queen is to _____**reign**_____ .
   a. reign   b. pursue   c. mutiny   d. modify

3. A scheme for cheating people is a _____**swindle**_____ .
   b. negative   c. singular   c. swindle   d. confederate

4. A claim of being elsewhere during a crime is a(n) _____**alibi**_____ .
   a. alibi   b. mutiny   c. discharge   d. reign

5. When you change plans slightly, you _____**modify**_____ them.
   a. modify   b. discharge   c. swindle   d. pursue

6. A person who freely expresses his or her opinion is _____**frank**_____ .
   a. confederate   b. economical   c. negative   d. frank

7. When you fire a gun, you _____**discharge**_____ it.
   a. swindle   b. discharge   c. pursue   d. modify

8. A person who is careful about spending money is _____**economical**_____ .
   a. frank   b. negative   c. economical   d. singular

9. A person who makes a suggestion that is not helpful is being _____**negative**_____ .
   a. economical   b. negative   c. frank   d. singular

10. A willing accomplice to a robbery is a(n) _____**confederate**_____ of the thief.
    a. confederate   b. alibi   d. discharge   d. mutiny

11. "I" is an example of a(n) _____**singular**_____ pronoun.
    a. negative   b. singular   c. confederate   d. economical

12. When you keep trying to achieve a goal, you _____**pursue**_____ it.
    a. modify   b. discharge   c. pursue   d. swindle

Synonyms

*For each item below choose the word that is most nearly the **same** in meaning as the word or phrase in **boldface**. Then write your choice on the line provided.*

1. a **blunt** answer to your question
   a. frank   b. negative   c. singular   d. confederate   _____ frank _____

2. **revise** the schedule
   a. discharge   b. pursue   c. modify   d. swindle   _____ modify _____

3. **aim for** a career in medicine
   a. modify   b. discharge   c. swindle   d. pursue   _____ pursue _____

4. an ironclad **excuse**
   a. confederate   b. reign   c. alibi   d. mutiny   _____ alibi _____

5. a **regime** of terror
   a. swindle   b. discharge   c. mutiny   d. reign   _____ reign _____

6. **cheated** by a con artist
   a. pursued   b. swindled   c. modified   d. discharged   _____ swindled _____

Antonyms

*For each item below choose the word that is most nearly **opposite** in meaning to the word or phrase in **boldface**. Then write your choice on the line provided.*

1. **positive** numbers
   a. negative   b. singular   c. economical   d. confederate   _____ negative _____

2. the **wasteful** use of natural resources
   a. frank   b. economical   c. singular   d. negative   _____ economical _____

3. soldiers who **obey**
   a. discharge   b. mutiny   c. reign   d. swindle   _____ mutiny _____

4. **load** a cannon
   a. modify   b. pursue   c. swindle   d. discharge   _____ discharge _____

5. **plural** nouns
   a. negative   b. economical   c. singular   d. frank   _____ singular _____

6. **enemies** of the tribe
   a. reigns   b. alibis   c. mutinies   d. confederates   _____ confederates _____

Completing the Sentence

From the list of words on pages 112–113, choose the one that best completes each item below. Write the word in the space provided. (You may have to change the word's ending.)

From the list of words on pages 112–113

EDITING AN ESSAY

■ When I write an essay, I start with a rough draft. Then I review what I have written to see how I can improve it. One way that I may _____**modify**_____ the essay is to get rid of any repetitions.

■ Because I want to keep the reader's attention, I try to keep my sentences clear and brief. Therefore, I look for more _____**economical**_____ ways to make my points.

■ For example, if I am writing about two people, I may want to use the plural pronoun *they* instead of _____**singular**_____ pronouns such as *he* and *she*. As a last step I reread the essay to make sure there are no errors of spelling, grammar, or punctuation.

TROUBLE ON THE HIGH SEAS

■ Captain William Bligh, an English admiral, _____**reigned**_____ over his ship, the *Bounty,* as if he were its king.

■ His harsh treatment and mean-spirited rules aroused _____**negative**_____ feelings among crew members. Few viewed the captain in a favorable light.

■ In a secret but _____**frank**_____ discussion, the sailors plotted to take over the ship.

■ A ship's officer named Fletcher Christian seized control of the *Bounty* on April 28, 1789. This daring _____**mutiny**_____ has been the subject of several popular movies.

CRIME AT THE CASH MACHINE

■ Soon after my uncle opened a checking account at a new bank, he was the victim of a bank machine _____**swindle**_____ .

■ A woman posing as a banker and her _____**confederate**_____ , who said he was the manager, advised my uncle to get $200 from the cash machine to test his bank card. The crooks then ran off with my uncle's money.

■ Using the descriptions given by my uncle and a witness, the police _____**pursued**_____ the two thieves on foot, catching up to them a few blocks away.

■ They soon arrested the suspects without having to _____**discharge**_____ their weapons.

■ At their trial the two thieves claimed that they were innocent. But the jury did not believe their _____**alibis**_____ . It took the jury only fifteen minutes to find them guilty.

Word Associations

Circle the letter next to the word or expression that best completes the sentence or answers the question. Pay special attention to the word in **boldface.**

1. A **frank** comment is
   a. always complimentary
   b. never hurtful
   c. always appreciated
   d. never dishonest

2. An **economical** car probably
   a. stalls frequently
   b. uses little gas
   c. pollutes the air
   d. runs on air

3. Infantry soldiers who **mutiny** are likely to
   a. get medals
   b. be promoted
   c. get new uniforms
   d. be punished

4. To **modify** a drawing you might
   a. erase a few lines
   b. crumple it up
   c. show it to a friend
   d. go to a museum

5. Which of these is a good **alibi**?
   a. "I didn't do it."
   b. "I was in school at that time."
   c. "I saw them rob the store."
   d. "I hope you catch the crook."

6. Which of these is a **singular** noun?
   a. chicks
   b. geese
   c. goose
   d. ducks

7. A **negative** person is likely to
   a. take great vacation pictures
   b. be good at math
   c. find fault with any plan
   d. see the best in everyone

8. A **reigning** king probably has
   a. boots and an umbrella
   b. a scepter and a crown
   c. a computer and a modem
   d. a bow and an arrow

9. If I **swindle** my little brother, I
   a. cheat him
   b. read to him
   c. protect him
   d. draw a picture of him

10. A factory is likely to **discharge**
    a. prisoners
    b. metal parts
    c. rifles
    d. smoke

11. I would expect my **confederates** to
    a. work together with me
    b. make fun of me
    c. refuse to help me
    d. plot against me

12. Which of these is a cat most likely to **pursue**?
    a. a dream
    b. a mouse
    c. a dog
    d. a career in television

UNIT 15

Definitions

Study the spelling, pronunciation, part of speech, and definition given for each of the words below. Write the word in the blank space in the sentence that follows. Then read the synonyms and antonyms.

1. **complicate**
   ('käm plə kāt)

   (v.) to make hard to understand or do
   A lot of unnecessary details sometimes can _____**complicate**_____ *directions.*

   SYNONYMS: to confuse, muddle, mix up
   ANTONYMS: to simplify, clarify, smooth, ease

2. **courteous**
   ('kər tē əs)

   (adj.) considerate toward others
   A _____**courteous**_____ *host is sure to greet all guests and make them feel welcome.*

   SYNONYMS: polite, well-mannered, respectful, civil
   ANTONYMS: rude, impolite, ill-mannered, discourteous

3. **discomfort**
   (dis 'kəm fərt)

   (n.) a lack of ease and well-being
   A nasty case of chicken pox can cause a great deal of _____**discomfort**_____.

   SYNONYMS: pain, distress, irritation, suffering
   ANTONYMS: comfort, peace, calm

4. **eliminate**
   (i 'li mə nāt)

   (v.) to get rid of or do away with
   If we all work together, we can _____**eliminate**_____ *hunger and poverty.*

   SYNONYMS: to remove, omit, leave out, exclude, drop
   ANTONYMS: to take in, admit, acquire, retain, preserve

5. **grieve**
   (grēv)

   (v.) to cause to feel great sadness; to feel very sad
   Reports of the many deaths and the destruction caused by the earthquake _____**grieve**_____ *us all.*

   SYNONYMS: to sadden, mourn, regret
   ANTONYMS: to rejoice, celebrate, gladden

6. **moral**
   ('môr əl)

   (adj.) having to do with what is right and wrong; being good and just
   A _____**moral**_____ *question is sometimes very difficult to answer.*

   (n.) the lesson taught by a story or experience
   I think that the _____**moral**_____ *of the story is "never give up."*

   SYNONYMS: honorable, upright, honest; a message, teaching
   ANTONYMS: immoral, wicked, bad, wrong

Millions of people visit New York every year to view the **spectacle** (word 9) of the Manhattan skyline.

7. **scorch**
(skôrch)

(v.) to burn on the surface; to dry out with heat
Did you _____scorch_____ my brand-new shirt with the iron?

(n.) a slight burn
I placed the napkin so it would cover a _____scorch_____ in the tablecloth.

SYNONYMS: to singe, brown, blacken, shrivel

8. **severe**
(sə 'vēr)

(adj.) of a serious nature; very strict and harsh; causing pain or hardship
Most parents think lying is a _____severe_____ offense.

SYNONYMS: grave, stern; tough, bitter; brutal, rough
ANTONYMS: unimportant; mild; merciful

9. **spectacle**
('spek ti kəl)

(n.) an unusual sight or public display
An eclipse of the sun is an awesome _____spectacle_____.

SYNONYMS: a scene, show, exhibition, marvel

10. **tragic**
('tra jik)

(adj.) having to do with a serious story with a sad ending; very unfortunate
Stories with _____tragic_____ endings make me cry.

SYNONYMS: dreadful, awful, sad, disastrous, unhappy
ANTONYMS: amusing, funny, humorous, comical, happy

11. **trifle**
('trī fəl)

(n.) something of little importance; a small amount
It is not worth arguing over such a _____trifle_____.

(v.) to treat carelessly or playfully
It is unkind to _____trifle_____ with someone's feelings.

SYNONYMS: a bit, knickknack, trinket; to fiddle, play, toy
ANTONYMS: a lot, lots of

12. **universal**
(yü nə 'vər səl)

(adj.) being everywhere; of, for, or shared by all
Food and shelter are _____universal_____ needs.

SYNONYMS: worldwide, broad, general, widespread
ANTONYMS: local, limited, narrow

Match the Meaning

For each item below choose the word whose meaning is suggested by the clue given. Then write the word in the space provided.

1. To feel great sadness over a loss is to _____**grieve**_____.
   a. scorch   b. trifle   c. grieve   d. eliminate

2. When you make a task harder, you _____**complicate**_____ it.
   a. complicate   b. eliminate   c. scorch   d. grieve for

3. If your throat is sore, you might feel _____**discomfort**_____.
   a. moral   b. discomfort   c. courteous   d. complicated

4. Joy that is shared by everyone in the world is _____**universal**_____.
   a. tragic   b. severe   c. universal   d. moral

5. Someone who is considerate of other people's feelings is _____**courteous**_____.
   a. courteous   b. moral   c. severe   d. tragic

6. During a dry spell the sun may _____**scorch**_____ the earth.
   a. complicate   b. eliminate   c. trifle with   d. scorch

7. A fatal accident is a _____**tragic**_____ event.
   a. moral   b. courteous   c. tragic   d. universal

8. A very strict or harsh king is a _____**severe**_____ ruler.
   a. universal   b. severe   c. courteous   d. tragic

9. A life that is good and just is a _____**moral**_____ one.
   a. moral   b. severe   c. tragic   d. universal

10. A small amount of something is a _____**trifle**_____.
    a. discomfort   b. moral   c. spectacle   d. trifle

11. To get rid of something is to _____**eliminate**_____ it.
    a. complicate   b. grieve for   c. trifle with   d. eliminate

12. A public display, such as fireworks, is a _____**spectacle**_____.
    a. trifle   b. spectacle   c. discomfort   d. moral

For each item below choose the word that is most nearly the **same** in meaning as the word or phrase in **boldface**. Then write your choice on the line provided.

1. caused great **distress**
   a. spectacle   b. trifle   c. discomfort   d. moral   _____discomfort_____

2. a grand **scene**
   a. moral   b. spectacle   c. trifle   d. discomfort   _____spectacle_____

3. the **message** of the fable
   a. trifle   b. scorch   c. spectacle   d. moral   _____moral_____

4. **burned** the grass
   a. scorched   b. eliminated   c. complicated   d. grieved for   _____scorched_____

5. **fiddle** with the rules
   a. complicate   b. scorch   c. eliminate   d. trifle   _____trifle_____

6. **leave out** the negative comments
   a. eliminate   b. complicate   c. trifle with   d. grieve for   _____eliminate_____

Antonyms

For each item below choose the word that is most nearly **opposite** in meaning to the word or phrase in **boldface**. Then write your choice on the line provided.

1. **simplify** things
   a. scorch   b. complicate   c. eliminate   d. trifle with   _____complicate_____

2. a **mild** winter
   a. severe   b. moral   c. universal   d. courteous   _____severe_____

3. having **limited** appeal
   a. tragic   b. severe   c. moral   d. universal   _____universal_____

4. **amusing** love stories
   a. universal   b. courteous   c. tragic   d. moral   _____tragic_____

5. a **rude** customer
   a. severe   b. universal   c. courteous   d. tragic   _____courteous_____

6. **rejoice** with the family
   a. trifle   b. grieve   c. scorch   d. eliminate   _____grieve_____

Completing the Sentence

From the list of words on pages 118–119, choose the one that best completes each item below. Then write the word in the space provided. (You may have to change the word's ending.)

DEATH OF A PRESIDENT

■ When President John F. Kennedy was killed by an assassin's bullet on November 22, 1963, the _____ **tragic** _____ event shocked the nation. The President was only forty-five years old.

■ Americans _____ **grieved** _____ openly as they watched his formal state funeral on television or listened to it on the radio.

■ People still recall the respectful and _____ **courteous** _____ behavior of the huge crowds that lined the funeral route.

WHY SAVE THE RAIN FORESTS?

■ The magnificent variety of animals and plants in the tropical rain forests creates a _____ **spectacle** _____ unlike anything else in nature.

■ The effort to protect these forests is _____ **complicated** _____ by the need to use some of the valuable resources found in them, such as medicines.

■ When any plant or animal is forever _____ **eliminated** _____ from the earth, the balance of nature changes. The loss of a single species may result in harm to many more.

■ One result of a change in the balance of nature can be a _____ **universal** _____ shift in weather patterns. A change that at first has only local effects may in time affect the whole world.

■ Many people now regard destruction of the rain forests as a _____ **moral** _____ issue, not just a political or legal one, because it can ruin the future of the entire planet.

SUNBURN REALLY HURTS

■ Many people do not realize how easily they can _____ **scorch** _____ their skin just by walking or playing outside on a sunny day.

■ Even on a cloudy day, it is possible to get a _____ **severe** _____ sunburn.

■ If you get a painful sunburn, ask your doctor what you should do to ease the _____ **discomfort** _____.

■ Always remember that a sunburn is nothing to _____ **trifle** _____ with. It can cause serious harm to your skin.

*Circle the letter next to the word or expression that best completes the sentence or answers the question. Pay special attention to the word in **boldface**.*

1. A **courteous** bus driver might
   a. yell at passengers
   b. greet each passenger
   c. wear gloves while driving
   d. pass your bus stop on purpose

2. A **severe** cold spell would
   a. cause great hardship
   b. delight all skiers
   c. make people sleepy
   d. not last long

3. A **tragic** event might make you
   a. jump for joy
   b. break a leg
   c. weep with sadness
   d. go to a show

4. If you feel **discomfort,** you should
   a. turn off the lights
   b. whistle in the dark
   c. rest for an hour
   d. seek relief

5. Which of these is a **universal** human experience?
   a. raising camels
   b. becoming an astronaut
   c. owning a rice plantation
   d. being born

6. Which is the **moral** of a story?
   a. "Slow and steady wins the race."
   b. "Do not fold, tear, or cut."
   c. "Dogs are related to wolves."
   d. "Why can't people fly?"

7. A **complicated** explanation is
   a. easy to understand
   b. likely to be false
   c. always helpful
   d. hard to follow

8. **Scorched** milk is sure to taste
   a. spicy
   b. sweet
   c. burnt
   d. refreshing

9. To **eliminate** sugar from your diet, you can
   a. add more salt
   b. learn how to cook
   c. cut out sweets
   d. drink lots of water

10. Which of these is a **trifle**?
    a. a party favor
    b. a huge weapon
    c. a million dollars
    d. a banquet

11. Which is a **spectacle**?
    a. a pair of glasses
    b. a three-ring circus
    c. an empty football field
    d. a bowl of vanilla ice cream

12. People usually **grieve** at
    a. birthday parties
    b. family funerals
    c. political rallies
    d. baseball games

Definitions

Study the spelling, pronunciation, part of speech, and definition given for each of the words below. Write the word in the blank space in the sentence that follows. Then read the synonyms and antonyms.

1. **assume**
   (ə 'süm)

   (v.) to take upon oneself; to take for oneself; to pretend to have or be; to take for granted
   My parents said I could have the puppy if I would _____assume_____ the responsibility for it.

   SYNONYMS: to accept, undertake, seize; to imagine, suppose, believe
   ANTONYMS: to reject, refuse, give up

2. **cram**
   (kram)

   (v.) to stuff tightly; to fill tightly; to study hard just before a test
   Mom told me not to _____cram_____ all my clothes into one drawer.

   SYNONYMS: to pack, crowd, jam, load, squeeze
   ANTONYMS: to empty, clean out, clear out

3. **endanger**
   (in 'dān jər)

   (v.) to expose to injury or harm
   Fire and drought _____endanger_____ our forests and the animals that live in them.

   SYNONYMS: to risk, threaten
   ANTONYMS: to protect, defend, preserve, save, secure

4. **fare**
   (fâr)

   (v.) to get along
   If you study hard, you should _____fare_____ well in school.

   (n.) the cost of travel on public transportation; food and drink
   Dad called to find out the plane _____fare_____ from Los Angeles to New York.

   SYNONYMS: to manage, succeed; a charge, fee, price, menu

5. **fertile**
   ('fər təl)

   (adj.) good for producing crops and plants; capable of developing or growing
   The rich farmland of the Midwest makes it one of the most _____fertile_____ areas in the world.

   SYNONYMS: fruitful, productive, rich
   ANTONYMS: barren, unproductive

6. **furnish**
   ('fər nish)

   (v.) to supply with furniture; to supply with what is needed
   After the fire damage was repaired, neighbors pitched in to help _____furnish_____ the house.

   SYNONYMS: to equip, outfit, provide, give
   ANTONYMS: to take, withhold

One of the most **fertile** (word 5) areas in the world is the Midwest, sometimes called "America's Breadbasket."

7. **mammoth**
('ma məth)

(n.) a very large, long-tusked, shaggy-haired elephant that is now extinct
The last woolly _____mammoth_____ died thousands of years ago.

(adj.) great in size
A skyscraper is a _____mammoth_____ building.

SYNONYMS: enormous, huge, immense, gigantic, colossal
ANTONYMS: small, tiny, little, miniature

8. **peer**
(pēr)

(n.) a person of the same age, rank, or ability; a British noble
As a gifted pianist, the child had no _____peer_____.

(v.) to look closely at
I tend to _____peer_____ at people through my glasses.

SYNONYMS: an equal, colleague; to gaze, stare, look, scan

9. **rigid**
('ri jəd)

(adj.) not bending; very strict
Stand at attention and keep your body _____rigid_____.

SYNONYMS: stiff, firm, inflexible; severe, stern
ANTONYMS: elastic, flexible, loose

10. **rowdy**
('raů dē)

(adj.) rough and disorderly
My teacher does not tolerate _____rowdy_____ behavior.

SYNONYMS: wild, unruly, noisy
ANTONYMS: quiet, tame, gentle, mild

11. **safeguard**
('sāf gärd)

(n.) something that protects
A helmet is a _____safeguard_____ against head injuries.

(v.) to protect against possible danger
Wear sunblock to _____safeguard_____ your skin.

SYNONYMS: a protection, defense; to defend, guard, save
ANTONYMS: to endanger, threaten, risk

12. **trespass**
(*n.,* 'tres pəs;
v., 'tres pas)

(n.) an action that is wrong; unlawful entry onto someone's property
The man was charged with criminal _____trespass_____.

(v.) to do wrong; to enter on someone's property without right
I did not mean to _____trespass_____ against you.

SYNONYMS: a sin, wrongdoing, invasion; to sin, offend, intrude

For each item below choose the word whose meaning is suggested by the clue given. Then write the word in the space provided.

1. If I put people at risk, I _____ endanger _____ their lives.
   a. cram   b. safeguard   c. assume   d. endanger

2. A noisy and wild party may be described as _____ rowdy _____ .
   a. mammoth   b. rowdy   c. fertile   d. rigid

3. A member of British royalty is a _____ peer _____ .
   a. peer   b. safeguard   c. mammoth   d. fare

4. To take something for granted is to _____ assume _____ it is so.
   a. cram   b. assume   c. furnish   d. endanger

5. When I eat bread and cheese for lunch, I dine on simple _____ fare _____ .
   a. safeguards   b. mammoths   c. fare   d. trespasses

6. A large, extinct "woolly" elephant is called a _____ mammoth _____ .
   a. mammoth   b. safeguard   c. peer   d. fare

7. If a lot of people get on a bus or train, they _____ cram _____ into it.
   a. furnish   b. assume   c. safeguard   d. cram

8. A person who is very strict may be described as _____ rigid _____ .
   a. rowdy   b. rigid   c. mammoth   d. fertile

9. If I protect people from risk, I _____ safeguard _____ their lives.
   a. assume   b. endanger   c. safeguard   d. furnish

10. An egg that can develop into a chick is one that is _____ fertile _____ .
    a. fertile   b. rowdy   c. mammoth   d. rigid

11. To enter someone's property without first getting permission is to _____ trespass _____ .
    a. cram   b. endanger   c. trespass   d. peer

12. If I supply necessary information, I _____ furnish _____ the facts.
    a. safeguard   b. endanger   c. assume   d. furnish

Synonyms

*For each item below choose the word that is most nearly the **same** in meaning as the word or phrase in **boldface**. Then write your choice on the line provided.*

1. **stare** through the window
   a. cram   b. trespass   c. peer   d. assume   _____ peer _____

2. **rich** soil
   a. rigid   b. fertile   c. rowdy   d. mammoth   _____ fertile _____

3. **defend** the planet
   a. furnish   b. endanger   c. cram   d. safeguard   _____ safeguard _____

4. collect the **fee**
   a. mammoth   b. fare   c. safeguard   d. peer   _____ fare _____

5. **equip** the lab
   a. furnish   b. endanger   c. cram   d. safeguard   _____ furnish _____

6. **intrude** on private property
   a. peer   b. assume   c. trespass   d. cram   _____ trespass _____

Antonyms

*For each item below choose the word that is most nearly **opposite** in meaning to the word or phrase in **boldface**. Then write your choice on the line provided.*

1. **small** in size
   a. rigid   b. mammoth   c. rowdy   d. fertile   _____ mammoth _____

2. a **quiet** activity
   a. rigid   b. fertile   c. mammoth   d. rowdy   _____ rowdy _____

3. a **flexible** rule
   a. mammoth   b. rowdy   c. fertile   d. rigid   _____ rigid _____

4. **empty** your locker
   a. furnish   b. safeguard   c. cram   d. endanger   _____ cram _____

5. **protect** the spotted owl
   a. cram   b. endanger   c. furnish   d. safeguard   _____ endanger _____

6. **give up** control
   a. furnish   b. safeguard   c. assume   d. endanger   _____ assume _____

Completing the Sentence

From the list of words on pages 124–125, choose the one that best completes each item below. Write the word in the space provided. (You may have to change the word's ending.)

A BIG MISTAKE

■ I made a big mistake when I _____**assumed**_____ that I could wait until the night before the big test to start studying. I should have known better than to take it for granted that I would do well on the test.

■ My _____**peers**_____ teased me when I told them that I was worried about the test. They said I didn't need to study hard. Now I know that I shouldn't have listened to them.

■ I had to stay up very late to _____**cram**_____ my brain full of facts and figures. When I realized how much I needed to learn, I began to feel sick with panic.

■ To make matters worse, the people in the house next door had a _____**rowdy**_____ party that lasted until one o'clock in the morning. I couldn't sleep because of the noise.

■ The next day I was so tired that I couldn't remember anything. So it was no surprise that I _____**fared**_____ badly on the test.

SAVE THE WETLANDS

■ America's wetlands provide a rich and _____**fertile**_____ environment for thousands of species of plants and animals.

■ But pollution and development more and more _____**endanger**_____ these beautiful places. In some areas their very survival is at risk.

■ If we lose our wetlands, many of the creatures that live there will become as extinct as the woolly _____**mammoth**_____.

■ Lots of concerned individuals and organizations are working to educate the public about how important it is to _____**safeguard**_____ this precious natural resource.

SAFETY IN A DANGEROUS PLACE

■ Scientists who study deadly viruses work in special laboratories where strict safety measures are enforced. There are _____**rigid**_____ rules to protect all the employees.

■ All workers are _____**furnished**_____ with special protective clothing that they must put on before going into the lab.

■ Only employees are allowed to enter the lab. Anyone who tries to get into one of these "hot zones" without proper identification will be considered to be _____**trespassing**_____. Security guards will escort intruders from the building.

Word Associations

Circle the letter next to the word or expression that best completes the sentence or answers the question. Pay special attention to the word in boldface.

1. A **fertile** animal may give birth to
   a. many young
   b. green plants
   c. good ideas
   d. fruits or vegetables

2. A jury of your **peers** would be made up of
   a. two dukes
   b. your parents
   c. other students
   d. telescopes

3. A **rowdy** greeting is likely to be
   a. stern
   b. loud
   c. gentle
   d. whispered

4. Which is a **safeguard** against theft?
   a. a burglar alarm
   b. sunscreen
   c. lifeguard
   d. deodorant soap

5. Which usually requires paying a **fare**?
   a. a skateboard ride
   b. a taxi ride
   c. a car ride
   d. a sled ride

6. One who **assumes** a brave manner is
   a. bragging
   b. fighting
   c. shouting
   d. pretending

7. A **crammed** suitcase is probably
   a. well organized
   b. half full
   c. hard to close
   d. locked

8. One way to say "No **Trespassing**" is
   a. "Closed for Repairs"
   b. "Keep Out"
   c. "Out of Business"
   d. "This Way to Exit"

9. If I **furnish** food for a picnic, I
   a. invite the ants
   b. set up the lawn furniture
   c. eat the lion's share
   d. bring lots to eat

10. A **mammoth** corporation probably has
    a. a large board of directors
    b. many elephants
    c. lions, tigers, and bears
    d. a small parking lot

11. An **endangered** species is
    a. threatened by extinction
    b. dangerous to others
    c. safe from harm
    d. protected by mammoths

12. Which of these is **rigid**?
    a. a rubber band
    b. a mound of jello
    c. a soap bubble
    d. a steel beam

Selecting Word Meanings

*For each of the following items circle the choice that is most nearly the **same** in meaning as the word in **boldface** type in the introductory phrase.*

1. an important scientific **achievement**
   a. failure   b. principle   c. method   d. accomplishment

2. **furnish** proof of ownership
   a. supply   b. copy   c. lose   d. request

3. an inexpensive **trifle**
   a. gift   b. trinket   c. dessert   d. weapon

4. a **singular** opportunity
   a. welcome   b. missed   c. unusual   d. lucky

5. a **moral** decision
   a. wicked   b. reasonable   c. just   d. difficult

6. arrested the **confederates**
   a. accomplices   b. witnesses   c. victims   d. enemies

7. **swindle** the tourist
   a. help   b. cheat   c. meet   d. entertain

8. **grieved** for the victims
   a. worked   b. rejoiced   c. searched   d. mourned

9. **endanger** the public's health
   a. ignore   b. protect   c. threaten   d. study

10. **sanitary** medical instruments
    a. filthy   b. sterile   c. new   d. used

11. an **economical** means of transportation
    a. thrifty   b. safe   c. comfortable   d. costly

12. a bitter **debate**
    a. medicine   b. person   c. taste   d. argument

Spelling

For each item below study the **boldface** word in which there is a blank. If a letter is missing, fill in the blank to make a correctly spelled word. If the word is already spelled correctly, leave the blank empty.

1. **spra_w_l** in a hammock
2. **tres___pass** on my land
3. **re_i_gn** over France
4. a **ro___wdy** mob
5. a **tra_g_ic** mistake
6. **a_c_quire** knowledge

7. a **fertil_e_** imagination
8. **s_c_orch** the linen
9. **safeg_u_ard** the passengers
10. a **mono___tonous** story
11. **mod_i_fy** the instructions
12. **elim_i_nate** the problem

Antonyms

For each of the following items circle the choice that is most nearly the **opposite** in meaning to the word in **boldface** type in the introductory phrase.

1. the **latter** part of the year
   a. earlier   b. warmest   c. last   d. largest

2. show signs of **discomfort**
   a. excitement   b. irritation   c. interest   d. calm

3. **cram** the theater aisles
   a. crowd   b. clear out   c. stand in   d. walk down

4. a **courteous** note
   a. unsigned   b. polite   c. short   d. rude

5. **preserve** the landmark building
   a. save   b. paint   c. destroy   d. enlarge

6. rise up in **mutiny**
   a. support   b. song   c. rebellion   d. anger

7. **complicate** the assignment
   a. confuse   b. complete   c. change   d. simplify

8. a **negative** attitude
   a. friendly   b. positive   c. bad   d. peculiar

Words have been left out of the following passage. For each numbered item in the passage, fill in the circle next to the word in the margin that best fills the blank space. Then answer each question below by writing a sentence that contains one of the words you have chosen.

In the decades following the Civil War, the poor were living in awful conditions in America's cities. Sickness, high infant death rates, poverty, and crime were __1__. Among the social reformers who dedicated themselves to changing this situation were Jacob Riis (1849–1914) in New York and Jane Addams (1860–1935) in Chicago.

1. ○ monotonous
   ○ frank
   ● widespread
   ○ mammoth

Riis shocked the nation with his book *How the Other Half Lives.* In it he described the terrible conditions in the slums of New York City. Legislators responded by passing laws aimed to __2__ the evils of tenement house life.

Jane Addams also devoted her talents to serving those in need. In a working-class neighborhood of Chicago, she founded Hull House to provide social services to the people who lived in the area, most of them immigrants. Among the __3__ of Addams and other reformers with whom she worked were the passage of the first juvenile court law, regulation of conditions in tenements, factory inspection, and worker's compensation. Like Jacob Riis, Jane Addams urged research into the causes of poverty and crime.

2. ● eliminate
   ○ complicate
   ○ exhibit
   ○ debate

3. ○ spectacles
   ○ alibis
   ○ swindles
   ● achievements

Addams also championed other important __4__ causes, including women's rights and justice for immigrants and African Americans.

4. ○ universal
   ● moral
   ○ sanitary
   ○ singular

5. What was one of the results of the work done in Chicago by Jane Addams?

   One of her **achievements** was the passage of the first juvenile court law.

6. What kind of causes did Addams work for?

   Addams championed important **moral** causes.

7. How common were poor living conditions in America's cities after the Civil War?

   Sickness, high infant death rates, poverty, and crime were **widespread**.

8. How did legislators respond to Riis's report of the terrible conditions in New York City?

   New York legislators responded by passing laws aimed to **eliminate** these evils.

Analogies

In each of the following circle the letter for the item that best completes the comparison. Then explain the relationship on the lines provided.

1. foe is to **friend** as
   a. ally is to buddy
   b. moral is to message
   c. night is to day
   d. rest is to relaxation

Relationship: "Foe" and "friend" are antonyms/opposite in meaning; "night" and "day" are antonyms/opposite in meaning.

2. humorous is to **tragic** as
   a. speedy is to quick
   b. prepared is to ready
   c. clean is to sanitary
   d. mammoth is to miniature

Relationship: "Humorous" and "tragic" are antonyms/opposite in meaning; "mammoth" and "miniature" are antonyms/opposite in meaning.

3. present is to **exhibit** as
   a. debate is to discuss
   b. reject is to accept
   c. stay is to leave
   d. fail is to succeed

Relationship: "Present" and "exhibit" are synonyms/the same in meaning; "debate" and "discuss" are synonyms/the same in meaning.

4. mouse is to **singular** as
   a. trap is to mouse
   b. mice is to plural
   c. mouse is to hole
   d. mice is to nice

Relationship: "Mouse" is the singular form; "mice" is the plural form.

Challenge: Make up your own

Write a comparison using the words in the box below. (Hint: There are four possible analogies.) Then write the relationship on the lines provided.

revolt	negative	eat	pencil
slaughter	fork	positive	mutiny
yes	massacre	write	no

Analogy: _____ is to _____ as _____ is to _____ .

Relationship: See Table of Contents

*The words in **boldface** in the sentences below are related to words introduced in Units 13–16. For example, the adjectives* trifling *and* spectacular *in item 1 are related to the nouns* trifle *and* spectacle *(both in Unit 15). Based on your understanding of the unit words that follow, circle the related word in **boldface** that best completes each sentence.*

assume	spectacle	courteous	pursue	furnish
rigid	modify	eliminate	trifle	rowdy
complicate	exhibit	severe	monotonous	moral
singular	tragic	preserve	universal	acquire

1. One reason for a movie's success at the box office may be its (**trifling/ spectacular**) special effects.

2. Several rooms in the museum display (**furnishings/complications**) from colonial America.

3. Scientists all over the world are working for the (**preservation/assumption**) of endangered animals such as the giant panda, the tiger, and the tamarins of the Amazon rain forests.

4. Americans believe that the (**courtesy/pursuit**) of happiness is a basic human right.

5. Because of the (**severity/rowdiness**) of the blizzard, highways were closed and flights were canceled.

6. Museum officials held a press conference to announce the (**modification/ acquisition**) of an important painting by Picasso.

7. Last fall my English class attended a performance of a (**tragedy/morality**) by William Shakespeare.

8. When I have a boring chore to do, I like to listen to music to relieve the (**monotony/singularity**) of the task.

9. A highlight of this year's science fair was an (**elimination/exhibition**) of crystals and minerals.

10. The popular author's new novel was widely praised for the (**universality/ rigidity**) of its story.

Use the clue and the given letters to complete each word. Write the missing letters of the word in the appropriate boxes. Then use the circled letters and the drawing to find the CHALLENGE word.

1. Rather unusual!

(S) I N G U L A (R)

2. An occasion for pro and con

D (E) B (A) T E

3. Another word for an English noble

(P) E E R

4. How would you describe a person who is polite and thoughtful?

C O U R T E O U (S)

5. Don't bother me with such an unimportant matter.

(T) R I F L E

6. A hospital operating room should always be this.

(S) A N I T A R Y

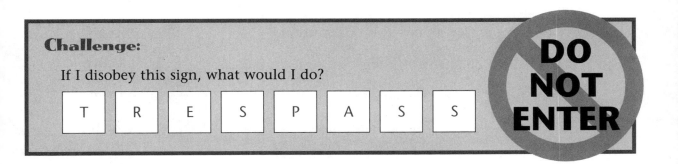

Challenge:

If I disobey this sign, what would I do?

T R E S P A S S

DO NOT ENTER

Definitions *Choose the word from the box that matches each definition. Write the word on the line provided.*

abolish	abuse	appeal	avalanche	brittle
dictator	displace	gauge	massacre	migrant
nestle	portable	preserve	rigid	scorch
selective	singular	spectacle	tragic	vicinity

1. an unusual sight or public display   spectacle

2. to settle down comfortably; to hold lovingly   nestle

3. not bending; very strict   rigid

4. a ruler or leader who has total power   dictator

5. to kill many people or animals in a cruel way   massacre

6. out of the ordinary   singular

7. the area near a place, the surrounding region   vicinity

8. to measure; to estimate   gauge

9. easily moved or changed   portable

10. improper, wrong, or cruel treatment   abuse

11. to force to move or flee; to move out of position   displace

12. very careful about choosing or using   selective

13. a sincere or strong request for something   appeal

14. to burn on the surface; to dry out with heat   scorch

15. very unfortunate   tragic

Antonyms

*Choose the word from the box that is most nearly **opposite** in meaning to each group of words. Write the word on the line provided.*

1. divided, separated; a foe   _confederate_

2. unlike, different   _identical_

3. to lose, give up, surrender   _acquire_

4. quiet, tame, gentle   _rowdy_

5. feast, plenty   _famine_

6. kindhearted, merciful   _pitiless_

7. to hate, despise, dishonor   _cherish_

8. local, limited, narrow   _universal_

9. to detain; to hire; to load   _discharge_

10. a defeat, failure, setback   _achievement_

11. barren, unproductive   _fertile_

12. to run away (from), flee   _pursue_

13. sensible, wise, intelligent   _absurd_

14. a hunter, predator   _prey_

15. wicked, bad, wrong   _moral_

16. to protect, defend, preserve   _endanger_

17. varied, lively, exciting   _monotonous_

18. to rejoice, celebrate, gladden   _grieve_

19. slow, dull, sluggish   _brisk_

20. to shrink, reduce, contract   _expand_

absurd
achievement
acquire
brisk
cherish
confederate
discharge
downfall
endanger
expand
famine
fertile
grieve
humiliate
identical
monotonous
moral
negative
pitiless
prey
pursue
rowdy
safeguard
security
universal

Completing the Sentence

Choose the word from the box that best completes each sentence below. Write the word in the space provided.

Group A

courteous	descend	economical	flimsy
latter	modify	navigate	rotate

1. Believe it or not, it may be harder to _____ **descend** _____ a steep hill than to climb it.

2. I carefully read the first part of the book, but I only skimmed the _____ **latter** _____ half.

3. You're not a true sailor until you are able to _____ **navigate** _____ choppy waters.

4. You're likely to feel cold if you wear a(n) _____ **flimsy** _____ jacket on a cool autumn night.

5. I waved to thank the _____ **courteous** _____ driver who let us cross the street.

Group B

alibi	confirm	fare	plea
principle	shred	soothe	trespass

1. I begged my parents to extend my curfew, but my _____ **plea** _____ fell on deaf ears.

2. My teacher will not accept "The dog ate my homework" as a(n) _____ **alibi** _____ for not handing in an assignment.

3. I'll call the airline to _____ **confirm** _____ our reservations so we'll be sure to have seats on the flight.

4. You'll need exact change to pay the _____ **fare** _____ when you board the bus.

5. Would you prefer creamy vanilla ice cream or hot tea with honey to _____ **soothe** _____ your sore throat?

Classifying

Choose the word from the box that goes best with each group of words. Write the word in the space provided. Then explain what the words have in common.

assume	daze	discomfort	foe	frank
mammoth	presentable	realistic	reign	tart

1. acceptable, enjoyable, _____presentable_____

   The words end with the same suffix.

2. dodo, passenger pigeon, saber-toothed tiger, _____mammoth_____

   The words name extinct animals.

3. bewilder, baffle, _____daze_____

   The words are synonyms.

4. real, _____realistic_____, reality, realize

   The words belong to the same family.

5. disorder, dishonor, _____discomfort_____

   The words begin with the same prefix.

6. blank, _____frank_____, sank, thank

   The words rhyme.

7. enemy, opponent, rival, _____foe_____

   The words are synonyms.

8. rain, rein, _____reign_____

   The words sound the same.

9. cookie, muffin, cake, _____tart_____

   The words name baked goods.

10. imagine, suppose, _____assume_____

    The words are synonyms.

Definitions For each item choose the word that matches the definition. Then write the word on the line provided.

1. to trick or lead a person into believing something that is not true
   a. blunder   b. displace   c. deceive   d. modify   **deceive**

2. weariness or exhaustion from work or lack of sleep
   a. feat   b. assault   c. discomfort   d. fatigue   **fatigue**

3. not correct; showing bad manners or taste
   a. improper   b. aggressive   c. severe   d. rigid   **improper**

4. to stun or confuse
   a. dispute   b. daze   c. gauge   d. debate   **daze**

5. easily broken or damaged, requiring special handling or care
   a. keen   b. flimsy   c. rigid   d. fragile   **fragile**

6. careful about spending money or using resources
   a. economical   b. moral   c. severe   d. energetic   **economical**

7. to cause to feel great sadness; to feel very sad
   a. enforce   b. justify   c. grieve   d. abuse   **grieve**

8. lasting or used for a limited time
   a. temporary   b. presentable   c. economical   d. moral   **temporary**

9. to stuff tightly; to fill tightly; to study hard just before a test
   a. distribute   b. bluff   c. classify   d. cram   **cram**

10. a discussion of reasons for and against something
    a. document   b. debate   c. plea   d. spectacle   **debate**

11. to plan or steer the course of a vessel or vehicle
    a. classify   b. emigrate   c. detect   d. navigate   **navigate**

12. a partner, friend
    a. confederate   b. associate   c. nomad   d. monarch   **associate**

13. easily broken, snapped, or cracked; not flexible
   a. tart   b. rigid   c. vivid   d. brittle   _____ brittle _____

14. to turn around a central point; to alternate
   a. flexible   b. rotate   c. alternate   d. navigate   _____ rotate _____

15. to show clearly; to put on display
   a. exhibit   b. detect   c. alternate   d. discharge   _____ exhibit _____

16. avoiding unnecessary risks or mistakes
   a. frank   b. moral   c. rowdy   d. cautious   _____ cautious _____

17. a friendly welcome and treatment of guests
   a. feat   b. hospitality   c. alibi   d. fare   _____ hospitality _____

18. to force obedience to
   a. acquire   b. dispute   c. ensure   d. enforce   _____ enforce _____

19. to make calm; to ease pain or sorrow
   a. soothe   b. cherish   c. blunder   d. gauge   _____ soothe _____

20. rough and disorderly
   a. energetic   b. shrewd   c. capable   d. rowdy   _____ rowdy _____

Parts of Speech   *For each item below indicate the part of speech of the word in* **boldface.** *In the space provided write* N *for noun,* V *for verb, or* A *for adjective.*

21. __N__ felt the **jolt**

22. __A__ a **supreme** effort

23. __V__ **shred** the evidence

24. __N__ joined the **mutiny**

25. __V__ **cancel** the reservations

26. __N__ fled the **famine**

27. __N__ settle the **dispute**

28. __A__ a **courteous** manner

29. __V__ **sprawl** on the couch

30. __A__ a **hearty** laugh

Completing the Sentence

Choose the word from the box that best completes each sentence. Write the word in the space provided. (You may have to change the word's ending.)

Group A

swindle	confirm	assume	postpone
reign	rigid	fertile	cherish

31. The mighty forces of nature can turn _____**fertile**_____ farmland into a wasteland in which nothing will grow.

32. I will always _____**cherish**_____ the memories of my visits to the Adirondacks.

33. It is the duty of the Senate to _____**confirm**_____ or reject the President's appointments to the Supreme Court.

34. A team that _____**reigns**_____ over a sport for several years is sometimes described as a "dynasty."

Group B

feat	scorch	reliable	vast
despise	strategy	preserve	blemish

35. The President promises to "_____**preserve**_____, protect, and defend the Constitution of the United States."

36. Although the fire had _____**scorched**_____ the letter, the writing could still be read.

37. It took many months for pioneers to cross the _____**vast**_____ stretches of the American plains.

38. The best _____**strategy**_____ for taking a test is to study hard so that you are as prepared for it as you can be.

39. A **spectacle** might make you
    a. sleep
    b. fall
    c. stare
    d. eat

40. On a **bluff** you might
    a. go for a swim
    b. enjoy the view
    c. do your homework
    d. call a friend

41. Which should we **condemn**?
    a. cruelty
    b. kindness
    c. breakfast
    d. humor

42. Your **foe** is *not*
    a. your enemy
    b. your opponent
    c. your challenger
    d. your friend

43. Where would a **monarch** sit?
    a. on a throne
    b. in a court
    c. in a classroom
    d. in a highchair

44. Texas is in the **vicinity** of
    a. Canada
    b. India
    c. Mexico
    d. Spain

45. To **peer**, you need
    a. eyes
    b. ears
    c. thumbs
    d. toes

46. Who needs an **alibi**?
    a. a plumber
    b. a doctor
    c. a farmer
    d. a burglar

47. Which might you **classify**?
    a. trading cards
    b. pizzas
    c. sunsets
    d. gifts

48. With an **avalanche** comes
    a. good news
    b. mail
    c. snow
    d. coupons

49. A **solitary** walk is one
    a. that you take at night
    b. that you take barefoot
    c. that you take alone
    d. that you take after dinner

50. Which runs in a **primary**?
    a. a chicken
    b. a candidate
    c. a horse
    d. a dog

INDEX

The following is a list of all the words taught in the units of this book. The number after each entry indicates the page on which the word is first introduced, but the word also appears in exercises on later pages.